Letts

GCSE
SUCCESS

VISUAL REVISION GUIDE

QUESTIONS & ANSWERS

ICT
INFORMATION & COMMUNICATION TECHNOLOGY

Author

Sean O'Byrne

CONTENTS

HOMEWORK DIARY

TOPIC	SCORE
Computer Systems	/38
Input and Output	/30
Storage Devices and Media	/24
The CPU	/30
Bits and Bytes	/32
Networks	/41
Networks – Layouts and Software	/29
Communication Methods	/30
Data Transfer	/30
Operating Systems 1	/30
Operating Systems 2	/32
Common Applications – Word Processing	/30
Common Applications – Database Software	/30
Common Applications – Database Management Software	/28
Common Applications – Spreadsheets	/30
Common Applications – DTP and Graphics	/30
Models and Simulations	/30
Data Logging and Control	/28
Tables, Fields and Records	/30
Data Capture	/34
Validation	/30
Data Capture and Validation	/34
Files	/35
File Processing	/30
Output	/33
Security	/30
Systems Development 1	/28
Systems Development 2	/30
Systems Development 3	/38
Documentation	/30
Algorithms and Flow Charts	/27
Computers and Work	/30
Effects of Information Technology	/30
Health and Safety	/29
Computer Misuse	/30
Data Protection Act	/30
Using the Internet	/29
Features of the Internet	/26
The Internet	/30
Drawbacks of the Internet	/28
Benefits of the Internet	/34

EXAM HINTS

- Try out lots of past papers. There is only so much that the exam can cover. Certain topics come up again and again, so looking at past papers gives you a good understanding of what examiners think is most important.

- Be organised.

- Do not repeat what is in the question. For example, if the question asks what is meant by reading and writing to memory, there is no point in saying data is written to and read from memory. You need to add something to what is said in the question to demonstrate that you really know what you are talking about. So, for this example, you might say that data is sent to memory or retrieved from memory by the processor.

- Look at the mark allocation. In many cases, one mark is given per point made. Sometimes, one mark is given for a fact, followed by another one for an explanation or example.

- Recognise the 'question' words. 'State' and 'Give' mean just put the fact down. 'Describe' or 'Explain' usually leads to a two-mark question, where some amplification of a basic fact is expected.

- Write neatly. Although marks are not actually deducted for bad writing, it is not in your interests to make the examiner struggle to interpret what you have written. Candidates who are careless with their writing are usually careless with their facts as well. If an answer cannot be read, it can only score zero.

- Do not write too much. Most GCSE papers provide spaces on the question papers for answers. They are designed to be about the right amount of space for what is required. If you end up needing additional sheets or writing in the margin spaces, you are writing too much! Remember – make the point and move on.

- Think in bullet points – marks are usually allocated per point made. The points do not have to be inside elaborate sentences. Even in longer questions, keep your answers concise.

- Never answer a question with words like 'easier', 'quicker', 'cheaper', 'more efficient' on their own. You need to say what is easier, quicker, etc.

- Use the scenario given in a question. Possibly what is required is just slightly different from the standard answers you have learned before: read the question carefully.

COMPUTER SYSTEMS

A

Choose just one answer, a, b, c or d.

1 Which of these items is not hardware?
(a) disk drive
(b) graphics card
(c) printer driver ✓✓
(d) motherboard   (1 mark)

2 In a washing machine, which is an input device?
(a) motor
(b) heater
(c) powder drawer
(d) keypad ✓✓   (1 mark)

3 The part of a computer where the programs are run is called the
(a) RAM ✓✗
(b) processor ✓

(c) ROM
(d) motherboard.   (1 mark)

4 Before a program can be run, it has to be
(a) loaded into RAM ✓✗
(b) loaded into ROM ✓✗
(c) stored on a disk
(d) stored in the processor.   (1 mark)

5 Any item of hardware connected to a computer processor unit is called
(a) an input device
(b) a peripheral ✓
(c) an output device ✓✗
(d) a storage unit. ✓✗   (1 mark)

Score 2 /5

B

Answer all parts of all questions.

1 Fill in the blanks.

Computer systems process the ....documents.... that has been given to them. They can be ....upgraded.... so that they can do many different jobs. Large computers are called ....mainter...., but these are often now replaced by many computers connected together in a ....connection.... (4 marks)

2 (a) Label the parts of this typical computer system.

A....floppy disk.... B....hard drive....

C....motherboard.... D....monitor....

```
[ A ] → [ B ] → [ C ]
            ↓
          [ D ]
```
(4 marks)

(b) On the diagram below, use the letters A, B, C and D in the same way, to point to the appropriate parts of the computer system.

(4 marks)

Score /12

C These are GCSE style questions. Answer all parts of the questions.

1 (a) Explain, with an example, what is meant by the term **hardware**.

Something you can touch and move with your hands ✓

(2 marks)

(b) Explain what is meant by the term **software**.

Some you can't touch ✓

(2 marks)

2 Parts of a computer's memory, or a certain file on disk, may be described as **read/write**. Explain what this means.

you can do either those things with this document

(3 marks)

3 (a) Explain what RAM is and what it is used for.

(5 marks)

(b) State **one** use for ROM.

loading a document ✓

(1 mark)

4 For the items in the following list, decide whether they are hardware or software and place them under the correct heading.

Windows   Hard disk controller
Payroll processing system Printer driver
RAM   Word processor
Network interface card   Processor

Hardware	Software
Printer driver ✗	windows ✓
Hard disk ✓	word processor ✓
Processor ✓	payroll
Network ✓	RAM ✗

(8 marks)

Score 10 /21

How well did you do?

0–13   Try again
14–19 Getting there
20–32 Good work
33–38 Excellent!

TOTAL SCORE 13 /38

For more on this topic
see pages 4–5 of your Success Guide

INPUT AND OUTPUT

A Choose just one answer, a, b, c or d.

1 Which of these could be an output device?
(a) mouse   (c) scanner
(b) joystick   (d) motor   (1 mark)

2 Which of these is an input device?
(a) monitor
(b) scanner
(c) printer
(d) loudspeaker   (1 mark)

3 What word can describe all of the following:
disk drive, printer, mouse, scanner?
(a) peripherals
(b) output devices
(c) input devices
(d) storage devices   (1 mark)

4 Which of these is an input device from which
items can be chosen from pictures?
(a) QWERTY keyboard
(b) concept keyboard
(c) monitor
(d) joystick   (1 mark)

5 Which of these is an alternative to a mouse,
sometimes found in laptop computers?
(a) joystick
(b) digitiser
(c) tracker ball
(d) graphics pad   (1 mark)

Score ☐ /5

B Answer all parts of all questions.

1 The following show examples of automated computer input methods. For each one, identify the method
and describe one advantage of that method.

(a)
MICHAEL F JAMSON   1001
124 OAKRIDGE DRIVE
YOUR CITY
WF12 123   DATE
Pay to the
order of _____ £
_____ POUNDS
YOUR FINANCIAL INSTITUTION
FOR _____   M
*094847933861 00011426633 1001

(c)
6794678423263

Method: ....
Advantage: ....

Method: ....
Advantage: ....

(b)
Halifax Airport
KINSMAN LOT   SHORT TERM PARKING AREA
KEEP THIS TICKET
CARS PARKED AT OWNERS RISK – LOCK YOUR CAR
895-609

(d)
Lottery
1 2 3 4 5 6
11 12 13 14 15 16
21 22 23 24 25 26
30 31 32 33 34 35

Method: ....
Advantage: ....

Method: ....
Advantage: ....   (8 marks)

2 Describe how a flat bed scanner can be used to produce a computer file.

....

....   (3 marks)

Score ☐ /11

C These are GCSE style questions. Answer all parts of the questions.

1 Terry is a student and he wants to buy a computer system. He needs it to find information for his homework and to print good quality work in colour, to hand in to his teachers.

Name **three** peripheral devices that he will need apart from a monitor, a keyboard and a mouse, and for each of these devices, explain why it is needed.

Device	Why needed
Printer	to print it at ✗ 2 2
motherboard	to get good graphics ✗
hard drive	to save his work ✗

(6 marks)

2 Amy is a garage owner. She needs a computer system to produce bills for her customers. These bills are printed on self-copying three-part paper. She also needs to print high quality leaflets to promote special offers such as a winter service.

Recommend **two** different types of printer to Amy and explain your reasons.

Ink jet print - to produce bills fast

high powered colour printer - to make it look pro ✓ professional

2

(4 marks)

3 A pub has a busy restaurant. The members of staff need to be able to enter which set meals customers have chosen and print out an itemised receipt when they have paid. Explain, with reasons, what input and output devices they will need.

....

....

....

....

0

(4 marks)

Score 4 /14

How well did you do?
0–10 Try again
11–15 Getting there
16–25 Good work
26–30 Excellent!

TOTAL SCORE 8 /30

**For more on this topic
see pages 6–7 of your Success Guide**

STORAGE DEVICES AND MEDIA

A Choose just one answer, a, b, c or d.

1 Which term can be used to describe a hard disk?
(a) storage device
(b) storage medium
(c) input device
(d) output device (1 mark)

2 Which term can be used to describe a DVD drive?
(a) storage device
(b) storage medium
(c) input device
(d) output device (1 mark)

3 A disk drive is an example of
(a) main storage
(b) an input device
(c) an output device
(d) backing storage. (1 mark)

4 A magnetised circle on a floppy disk is called
(a) a sector
(b) a cylinder
(c) a block
(d) a track. (1 mark)

5 How much data can a floppy disk store?
(a) 1.44Mb
(b) 1.44Gb
(c) 1.44Kb
(d) 1024 bytes. (1 mark)

Score /5

B Answer all parts of all questions.

1 State two reasons why a floppy disk might be chosen for file storage.

....

.... (2 marks)

2 Explain what is meant by a cylinder on a hard disk.

.... (2 marks)

3 On the diagrams of a magnetic disk, state what the arrows indicate.

(a)

....

(b)

.... (2 marks)

Score /6

C These are GCSE style questions. Answer all parts of the questions.

1 Liam has put a floppy disk into the drive of his computer to save some work that he needs to take home. The computer gives him a message which says 'this disk is not formatted; do you want to format it now?'

(a) Explain in detail what the computer will do if he replies 'OK'.

....

....

....

(3 marks)

(b) Liam successfully formats the disk. He has written a long document with his word processor and it contains lots of embedded pictures, pasted from the Internet. He still cannot save his work onto the floppy disk. Explain why.

....

....

(3 marks)

2 A travel agent is working on-line, checking an airline's flight timetables and making a booking for a client. The booking details are held on a backing storage device owned by the airline.

(a) What type of storage device would have to be used by the airline?

....

(1 mark)

(b) Explain why it is necessary to use this sort of device.

....

....

(3 marks)

3 A software company distributes its products on CDs. Explain why CDs are suitable for this purpose.

....

....

(3 marks)

Score /13

How well did you do?

0–8 Try again
9–12 Getting there
13–20 Good work
21–24 Excellent!

TOTAL SCORE /24

For more on this topic see pages 8–9 of your Success Guide

11

THE CPU

A

Choose just one answer, a, b, c or d.

1 An AND gate gives an output if
(a) 2 inputs at the same time are different
(b) a pulse is followed by no pulse
(c) 2 inputs at the same time are the same
(d) 2 pulses occur in quick succession.
(1 mark)

2 The speed of a processor can be measured in
(a) megabytes
(b) gigabytes
(c) megahertz
(d) kilobytes. (1 mark)

3 What device is used to input data into a burglar alarm system?
(a) scanner (c) light pen
(b) sensor (d) reader. (1 mark)

4 Modern computers are all based on digital technology. This means that the data is
(a) handled by varying the electrical voltage
(b) stored as a set of decimal numbers
(c) always stored using ASCII code
(d) handled as on/off electrical signals.
(1 mark)

5 Which of these is carried out by a microprocessor?
(a) storage of a program
(b) adding two numbers together
(c) storage of data while it is being sent to a peripheral
(d) holding a disk file directory. (1 mark)

Score /5

B

Answer all parts of all questions.

1 Fill in the blanks.

(a) The part of a computer that carries out the program instructions is called the ....
This part can also move data from one .... to another. This part of the computer is constructed on a small piece of .... (3 marks)

(b) When a program is loaded, it is copied from .... into .... When it is running, each instruction is copied to the .... , where it will be ....
and .... (5 marks)

2 Briefly explain the purpose of logic circuits. ....
.... (2 marks)

3 Explain how a computer's clock speed can affect the running of a program.

....

.... (2 marks)

4 This question refers to different logic gates. Would an output result when:

OUTPUT (Y/N)

(a) an AND gate receives two impulses at the same time? ☐

(b) an AND gate receives one input? ☐

(c) an OR gate receives two inputs at the same time? ☐

(d) a NOT gate receives an input? ☐ (4 marks)

Score /16

C These are GCSE style questions. Answer all parts of the questions.

1 A washing machine has a logic circuit set up as follows:

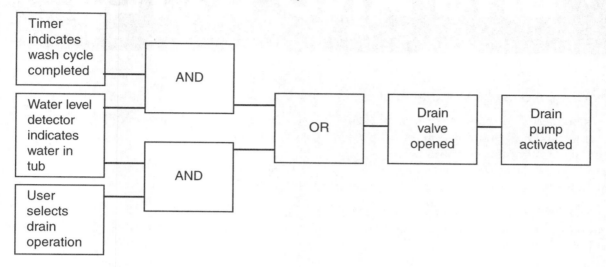

Describe what happens if:

(a) the user selects "drain" but there is no water in the tub?

....

(b) the wash cycle is completed and there is water in the tub?

....

(c) the wash cycle is completed, there is no water in the tub and the user selects the drain operation?

....

(d) the wash cycle is completed and there is no water in the tub?

.... (4 marks)

2 Here are some of the actions that take place while a computer program is running:

(a) an instruction is copied to the processor

(b) an instruction is carried out

(c) the program's instructions are copied from disk into RAM

(d) an instruction is decoded

(e) an instruction is copied onto the data bus

Order	Event
1	
2	
3	
4	
5	

Place these events in the table in their correct order. (5 marks)

Score /9

How well did you do?

0–10	Try again
11–15	Getting there
16–25	Good work
26–30	Excellent!

TOTAL SCORE /30

For more on this topic see pages 10–11 of your Success Guide

BITS AND BYTES

A

Choose just one answer, a, b, c or d.

1 If a sentence is stored in ASCII format, how much disk space would be taken by the sentence 'Programming is fun.'?
(a) 19 bytes   (c) 17 bytes
(b) 18 bytes   (d) 16 bytes.   (1 mark)

2 Modern computers are all based on digital technology. This means that the data is
(a) handled by varying the electrical voltage
(b) stored as a set of decimal numbers
(c) handled as on/off electrical signals
(d) always stored using ASCII code.   (1 mark)

3 1 megabyte of memory contains
(a) 1,024 gigabytes
(b) 1,024 bytes
(c) 1,000,000 bytes
(d) 1,024 kilobytes.   (1 mark)

4 The amount of data stored in one memory location is
(a) 1 bit
(b) 1 kilobyte
(c) 1 byte
(d) 1 megabyte.   (1 mark)

5 A floppy disk can store 1.44 MB. This is the same as
(a) 1,440 K
(b) 1,474.56 K
(c) 1,509,949.44 K
(d) 14.4 K.   (1 mark)

Score   /5

B

Answer all parts of all questions.

1 Fill in the blanks.

(a) Computers are often required to store characters. One way is to use the ASCII system. The letters ASCII stand for .... In ASCII, characters are represented by .... Another system used to store characters is called .... and it can store many more different characters than ASCII.   (3 marks)

(b) The smallest amount of data that can be stored in a computer is one .... This is short for .... Eight of these make up one ....   (3 marks)

2 In a computer, data is stored as a series of zeros and ones. What is the name given to a number system based on just zeros and ones?
....   (1 mark)

3 List three different types of data that can be stored in a computer's RAM.
....   (3 marks)

4 Explain how the computer can distinguish between different types of data when they are all stored in the same way.
....   (1 mark)

Score   /11

C **These are GCSE style questions. Answer all parts of the questions.**

1 Ben wants to buy a PC. The salesperson tells him that he needs at least 256 MB of RAM.

(a) How much memory is this in kilobytes?

.... (1 mark)

(b) When Ben is using his PC, state four items that are likely to be stored in RAM?

.... (4 marks)

(c) Ben needs to insert a lot pictures into his word-processed documents. The salesperson tells Ben that he needs as much RAM as possible. Explain why a lot of RAM is needed to store a picture.

....

.... (4 marks)

(d) Ben wants to record and edit some moving images to put on his website. The salesman recommends that he needs to buy a CD rewriter as well. Explain why he may need this in these circumstances.

....

.... (3 marks)

2 Characters can be stored in a computer system using the ASCII system. If the ASCII code for 'A' is 65, what does 66, 89, 84, 69 represent?

.... (2 marks)

3 Data is encoded in a computer by means of switches being set. Explain how a switch can be used to represent data.

.... (2 marks)

Score   /16

How well did you do?

0–10   Try again
11–16 Getting there
17–26 Good work
27–32 Excellent!

TOTAL SCORE   /32

**For more on this topic
see pages 12–13 of your Success Guide**

NETWORKS

A Choose just one answer, a, b, c or d.

1 A workstation is connected to a network by
(a) a network interface card
(b) a hub
(c) a switch
(d) a router. (1 mark)

2 Which of these types of network cable is not affected by interference from other cables?
(a) UTP
(b) co-axial
(c) fibre-optic
(d) thin Ethernet (1 mark)

3 Which of these devices allows many computers to connect to a server's network interface card?
(a) router
(b) switch
(c) modem
(d) bridge (1 mark)

4 A computer network that is confined to one site is called a
(a) MAN
(b) LAN
(c) WAN
(d) peer-to-peer. (1 mark)

5 A company provides its users with a network that can be accessed from all its offices world-wide. This network is
(a) a LAN
(b) a MAN
(c) a WAN
(d) an intranet. (1 mark)

Score   /5

B Answer all parts of all questions.

1 (a) Explain the difference between a LAN and a WAN.

....

.... (2 marks)

(b) Describe what differences there are likely to be in the way computers are connected in a LAN and in a WAN.

LAN: ....

WAN: .... (3 marks)

(c) (i) A university has many buildings spread out over a campus. State what type of network would link its computers together.

.... (1 mark)

(ii) State the type of cabling that the university would be most likely to use to make connections between different buildings and explain the reasons for this choice.

....

.... (3 marks)

2 On a particular network, one computer is used to store the data shared by all the users. State what this computer is called.

.... (1 mark)

Score   /10

C **These are GCSE style questions. Answer all parts of the questions.**

1 Chris works from home and does a lot of work on his computer, programming and writing documentation. He decides that it would be a good idea if he were to install his own network.

(a) Explain **three** advantages that Chris would gain from having a network.

....

.... (3 marks)

(b) Explain **three** disadvantages of setting up such a network.

....

.... (3 marks)

(c) Apart from the usual computers and peripherals, describe **three** extra items of hardware that Chris might have to obtain in order to set up his network. State the purpose of each component.

....

.... (6 marks)

(d) Chris wants to connect his network to the Internet. He considers using a modem for this purpose. Explain the purpose of a modem.

.... (3 marks)

(e) He decides instead to connect to an ISDN line. Explain why this can be a better choice than using a modem and why no modem is required for an ISDN link.

.... (3 marks)

2 A small company designs the layouts for books. It employs three designers who use desktop publishing software to arrange the text and illustrations that they receive by e-mail from the authors. A secretary uses office software for administrative purposes. The company is planning to install a network with six workstations and two servers.

(a) Explain, with examples, why this company might require two servers rather than just one.

....

.... (3 marks)

(b) State **two** ways in which the network will allow the company to improve the security of its data files.

.... (2 marks)

(c) (i) Explain why the company might now need to appoint an extra member of staff.

.... (1 mark)

(ii) Describe what the role of this person would be.

.... (2 marks)

Score /26

How well did you do?

0–14 Try again
15–20 Getting there
21–34 Good work
35–41 Excellent!

TOTAL SCORE /41

For more on this topic see pages 14–15 of your Success Guide

17

NETWORKS – LAYOUTS AND SOFTWARE

A

Choose just one answer, a, b, c or d.

1 When a user on a network prints a file, it goes into a print queue just before printing. Where is this queue held?
(a) on the server's hard disk
(b) in the server's RAM
(c) on the client's hard disk
(d) in the client's RAM (1 mark)

2 On a network, a payroll clerk needs only to be able to view personnel records. A suitable level of access to these files would be
(a) read/write (c) execute
(b) read-only (d) delete. (1 mark)

3 A workstation on a network is also called
(a) a server (c) a terminal
(b) a hub (d) a client machine.
(1 mark)

4 A small network that does not have a server is called
(a) a peer-to-peer network
(b) a ring network
(c) a star network
(d) a bus network. (1 mark)

5 One type of network has all the devices connected to one common cable with a terminator at each end. This is called
(a) a ring network
(b) a bus network
(c) a star network
(d) a peer-to-peer network. (1 mark)

Score /5

B

Answer all parts of the question.

1 The diagram below shows the layout of one particular type of network.

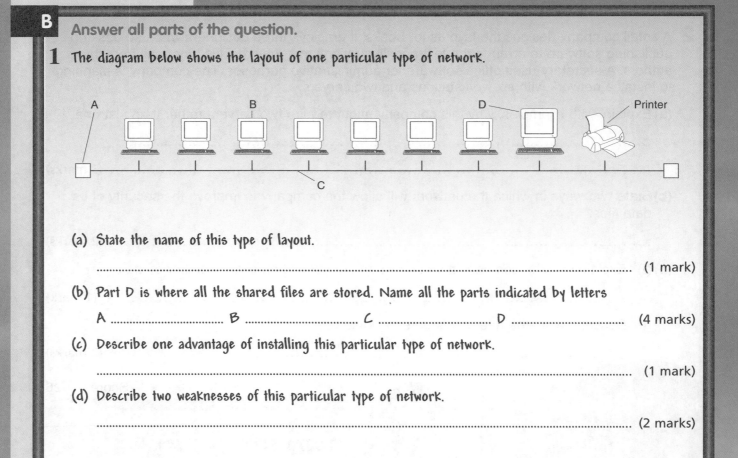

(a) State the name of this type of layout.

.... (1 mark)

(b) Part D is where all the shared files are stored. Name all the parts indicated by letters

A .... B .... C .... D .... (4 marks)

(c) Describe one advantage of installing this particular type of network.

.... (1 mark)

(d) Describe two weaknesses of this particular type of network.

.... (2 marks)

Score /8

C   These are GCSE style questions. Answer all parts of the questions.

A small firm of insurance brokers is considering installing a network. One of the options they consider is a peer-to peer layout.

1 Explain what a peer-to-peer network is.

....

....   (2 marks)

2 Explain why this type of network may be suitable in this situation.

....

....

....   (3 marks)

3 A client-server system is chosen instead. Network software is installed on all the computers. The server has multitasking software installed.

   (a) Explain what is meant by **multitasking**.

   ....

   ....   (2 marks)

   (b) Explain why **multitasking software** is necessary on a server machine.

   ....

   ....   (2 marks)

   (c) State **two** advantages of using a client-server network layout.

   ....

   ....   (2 marks)

4 The server software has many security features. State **three** of these features.

....

....

....   (3 marks)

5 Explain the purpose of logging on.

....

....   (2 marks)

Score   /16

How well did you do?

0–9	Try again
10–14	Getting there
15–24	Good work
25–29	Excellent!

TOTAL SCORE   /29

For more on this topic
see pages 16–17 of your Success Guide

COMMUNICATION METHODS

A

Choose just one answer, a, b, c or d.

1 A mobile telephone that is able to access Internet pages uses which of these protocols?
(a) FTP   (c) WAP
(b) SMP   (d) IPX   (1 mark)

2 An advantage of using the telephone instead of e-mail is
(a) with telephone messages, the person is reached immediately
(b) e-mails can often be misunderstood
(c) telephone calls are cheaper than e-mails
(d) telephone conversations are completely private.   (1 mark)

3 An advantage of e-mail is
(a) it can be accessed from any connected computer in the world
(b) it is totally secure
(c) you only receive the communications that you want
(d) it costs nothing to send.   (1 mark)

4 Why is it a good idea not to open e-mails from unknown sources?
(a) opening them will lead to more junk e-mail
(b) opening them will waste space on your hard disk
(c) opening them may reveal passwords to others
(d) they may carry a virus   (1 mark)

5 Video conferencing is often of poor quality when Internet connectivity is used. The most likely reason for this is
(a) the internet cannot send moving pictures
(b) many users do not have broadband connections
(c) the operating system of many PCs is incompatible with video conferencing
(d) web cameras do not have enough pixel density.   (1 mark)

Score   /5

B

Answer all parts of all questions.

1 (a) State four reasons why e-mail is often preferred over other methods of communication.

.... (4 marks)

(b) Describe two drawbacks of e-mail.

.... (2 marks)

2 Describe three reasons why a business may want to communicate with its customers via web pages.

.... (3 marks)

3 Explain why video conferencing is best achieved with a broadband connection.

....

....

....

....

....

(4 marks)

Score   /13

C These are GCSE style questions. Answer all parts of the questions.

1 A business traveller is staying in a hotel in England. He has to keep in touch with his office from time to time. His son is back-packing in Australia. Many methods of communication are available. For each of the following situations, state a suitable method of communication and give a reason for your choice.

Situation	Suitable method of communication	Reason
Sending a message to his son		
Discussing a customer's account with the sales manager		
Demonstrating a product to a number of customers in different locations		
Sending a spreadsheet file to head office		

(8 marks)

2 Explain **two** reasons why a home can benefit from connection to satellite communication systems.

....

.... (4 marks)

Score   /12

How well did you do?

0–10   Try again
11–15   Getting there
16–25   Good work
26–30   Excellent!

TOTAL SCORE   /30

**For more on this topic
see pages 18–19 of your Success Guide**

DATA TRANSFER

A Choose just one answer, a, b, c or d.

1 Broadband network connection means
(a) more bits of data are transmitted per second
(b) thicker cables are used
(c) more cables are used
(d) fibre-optic cables are used. (1 mark)

2 The reason why image files are often compressed on Internet sites is
(a) the image quality is improved
(b) they transmit faster
(c) fewer pixels are used in the display
(d) browsers can only display compressed images. (1 mark)

3 Which of these could improve the response time of a network?
(a) change to a bus network topology
(b) increase client disk space
(c) add an extra hub
(d) give the server more RAM (1 mark)

4 A person often wants to download music from the Internet but finds it too slow. The best way to reduce download times would be to
(a) change to a different ISP
(b) install more RAM
(c) install a broadband connection
(d) increase hard disk space. (1 mark)

5 It is a good idea to limit the amount of graphics on a web page. Which of these facts is relevant?
(a) most surfers have small amounts of RAM
(b) some surfers use ISDN
(c) some surfers have broadband connections
(d) most surfers use modems (1 mark)

Score   /5

B Answer all parts of all questions.

1 (a) Data is often sent over networks in a compressed form. Explain what this means and the advantage of doing it.

.... (2 marks)

(b) The following are commonly used compression standards. For each one, state what sort of file is being compressed.

Standard	Type of file
jpeg	
gif	
mpeg	

2 Explain why it is often a good idea to limit the amount of graphics used on a web page. (3 marks)

....

.... (4 marks)

3 (a) A modem is advertised as being 56 Kbps. How long is the shortest time that it would take to download a file of 1 MB? Show your working.

.... (3 marks)

(b) In practice, the 1 MB file may take longer than this to download. Explain one reason why this might be the case.

.... (2 marks)

Score   /14

C These are GCSE style questions. Answer all parts of the questions.

1 A small college uses a 3-station client-server network for its administration. The computers are connected by a bus cable. Recently, with increasing student numbers, the office staff have noticed that the network performance has slowed down.

Explain how each of the following factors may influence network performance and how changes can be made to improve the network's speed.

(a) network topology (layout)

.... (2 marks)

(b) the network cards

.... (2 marks)

(c) the specification of the server

.... (2 marks)

2 Explain why network performance can be improved by storing commonly used applications on local hard drives rather than on the server.

....
.... (2 marks)

3 An ISP needs to have servers with a high specification. Explain what this means and why it is important in this case.

....
....
.... (3 marks)

Score   /11

How well did you do?

0–10	Try again
11–15	Getting there
16–25	Good work
25–30	Excellent!

TOTAL SCORE **/30**

For more on this topic see pages 20–21 of your Success Guide

OPERATING SYSTEMS 1

A Choose just one answer, a, b, c or d.

1 Which of these tasks would be best suited to run under a batch processing operating system?
(a) monitoring a patient's heart rate
(b) producing electricity bills
(c) guiding an aircraft
(d) arranging hotel bookings   (1 mark)

2 An operating system lets the user group files together for convenience. Such a group is called
(a) a sector   (c) a directory
(b) a cluster   (d) a block.   (1 mark)

3 Which of these situations is most likely to require scheduling from the operating system?

(a) real-time   (c) single program
(b) single user   (d) multitasking   (1 mark)

4 Which of these situations would be best suited to a real-time operating system?
(a) printing wage slips
(b) processing exam marks
(c) a computer game
(d) making a weather forecast from weather data   (1 mark)

5 Some operating systems require the user to type in instructions to the computer. The software that allows the computer to understand these instructions is called
(a) a command interpreter
(b) a compiler
(c) an assembler
(d) a loader.   (1 mark)

Score   /5

B Answer all parts of all questions.

1 Here are some examples of processes that may be carried out by a computer:

A working out exam grades
B sending output to a printer
C finding space in memory for a program

D keeping an aircraft on course
E writing a letter
F making a list of overdue videos in a video shop.

Write each of the letters A-F in the correct column of the table according to whether the process is carried out by an application or the operating system.

Application	Operating system

(6 marks)

2 Fill in the blanks.

When a computer is first switched on, the operating system is loaded from the .... into .... This process is called .... Once loaded, the operating system allows the user to control the .... of the computer system.   (4 marks)

3 Explain how an operating system can give the illusion of running more than one program at once.

....

....

(3 marks)

Score /13

C These are GCSE style questions. Answer all parts of the questions.

1 When using a computer network, it is necessary to log in.

(a) State **two** reasons why this is necessary.

....

.... (2 marks)

☐ **Login**   ☒

User Name: lettsf

Password: xxxxxxxxxxx

           OK   Cancel

(b) State two resources that are likely to be shared by different users on a network.

....

.... (2 marks)

2 (a) Explain what is meant by a disk **directory**.

....

.... (2 marks)

(b) Most disk directories are organised in a **tree** structure. Explain what this means.

.... (1 mark)

3 (a) Explain what is meant by a real-time operating system.

....

.... (2 marks)

(b) Describe **one** situation where a real-time operating system is necessary.

.... (1 mark)

(c) Explain why a real-time operating system is necessary in this case.

.... (2 marks)

Score   /12

How well did you do?

0–10   Try again
11–15 Getting there
16–25 Good work
26–30 Excellent!

TOTAL SCORE   /30

**For more on this topic
see pages 24–25 of your Success Guide**

OPERATING SYSTEMS 2

A

Choose just one answer, a, b, c or d.

1 A small single purpose program is called
(a) an application (c) an operating system
(b) a utility (d) a procedure. (1 mark)

2 Which of these statements about GUIs is true?
(a) They are harder to use than CLIs.
(b) They do not allow many programs to be held in RAM at the same time.
(c) It is easy to set up batch files to configure them.
(d) They need more RAM than CLIs.
(1 mark)

3 The software used by the operating system to communicate with a peripheral is called
(a) a driver
(b) a utility

(c) an interface
(d) an application. (1 mark)

4 The display in a GUI is stored as
(a) a compressed image
(b) a bit-mapped graphic
(c) a vector graphic
(d) a character map. (1 mark)

5 A GUI represents a program with a picture. This picture is called
(a) a menu
(b) a control
(c) an icon
(d) a button. (1 mark)

Score /5

B

Answer all parts of all questions.

1 The manager of a network can choose to work with a graphical user interface (GUI) or a command line interface (CLI). He prefers to do most of his work using a CLI.

(a) Explain how a user operates a computer with a CLI.

....
.... (2 marks)

(b) Explain why the network manager often prefers to use a CLI.

....
....
.... (3 marks)

2 State four file operations that you can carry out using operating system utilities.

....
.... (4 marks)

3 Describe what is meant by

(a) pointing and clicking .... (2 marks)

(b) dragging and dropping .... (2 marks)

Score /13

C These are GCSE style questions. Answer all parts of the questions.

1 **(a)** Explain what is meant by a computer **interface**.

....

.... (2 marks)

(b) List **four** features you would expect to find in a GUI.

....

....

....

.... (4 marks)

(c) Most computer systems sold to home users come with a GUI installed. Explain why most users prefer to work with a GUI.

....

.... (2 marks)

2 Bill loads the latest GUI-based operating system onto his old computer. He finds that the machine runs extremely slowly. His friend tells him that he would get a better performance from his machine if he installed extra RAM and a faster processor.

Explain why his friend gives this advice.

....

....

....

.... (4 marks)

3 This is an illustration of a feature in a user interface.

(a) State the name of this feature interface.

.... (1 mark)

(b) Explain the purpose of this type of feature.

....

....

....

.... (2 marks)

Score /14

How well did you do?
0–11 Try again
12–17 Getting there
18–27 Good work
28–32 Excellent!

TOTAL SCORE **/32**

**For more on this topic
see pages 26–27 of your Success Guide**

27

COMMON APPLICATIONS – WORD PROCESSING

A Choose just one answer, a, b, c or d.

1 A typist wants to change many occurrences of one word to another. The most efficient way to do this is to
(a) produce a macro
(b) use the search and replace facility
(c) change the template
(d) change the style. (1 mark)

2 A word processor lets you create a standard combination of text features such as font, size and colour. This combination can then be applied to any text. This is called
(a) a template   (c) a style
(b) a macro   (d) a format. (1 mark)

3 An advantage of using off-the-shelf software is
(a) it is specially adapted to your requirements
(b) it requires no customising
(c) it is easy to contact the programmer for help
(d) it is available immediately. (1 mark)

4 Which of these is an example of generic software?
(a) atmosphere modelling
(b) insurance premium calculator
(c) a word processor
(d) traffic light control. (1 mark)

5 When using a word processor, a mouse cursor is positioned over an item and then moved while holding down the left button. The button is then released. This is called
(a) drag and drop   (c) search and replace
(b) point and click (d) cut and paste. (1 mark)

Score   /5

B Answer all parts of all questions.

1 (a) Explain what is the meaning of the term generic software.

....

.... (2 marks)

(b) Enter the following types of software into the table, according to whether they are generic or special purpose software packages.

- Traffic light control
- Desktop publishing
- Web browser
- Automatic camera control
- Spreadsheet
- Insurance premium calculations

Generic	Special purpose

(6 marks)

2 Give three reasons why a spell checker might report a word as incorrect, when it is in fact correct.

....

....

.... (3 marks)

Score   /11

28

These are GCSE style questions. Answer all parts of the questions.

1 Explain what is meant by **mail-merge**.

....

.... (3 marks)

2 The system flow chart below shows the process of mail-merging a letter. The first box is labelled.

Type letter

Label the other boxes with the correct words from the list below.

- data file   • letter file
- letter   • print letter
- merge   (5 marks)

3 Sarah runs a small business, designing and printing DVD box covers. She uses a generic software package to help in her work. The software contains a number of component parts. Describe how **three** of the parts of this software could be used to help in her business.

....

....

.... (6 marks)

Score   /14

How well did you do?

0–10	Try again
11–15	Getting there
16–25	Good work
26–30	Excellent!

TOTAL SCORE   /30

**For more on this topic
see pages 28–29 of your Success Guide**

COMMON APPLICATIONS – DATABASE SOFTWARE

A

Choose just one answer, a, b, c or d.

1 A database consisting of only one table is called
  (a) a relational database
  (b) a hierarchical database
  (c) a network database
  (d) a flat file database. (1 mark)

2 When creating a database application, the user interface is produced by using
  (a) reports
  (b) forms
  (c) queries
  (d) modules. (1 mark)

3 Which of the following data items would be suitable for use as a key field?
  (a) customer reference number
  (b) customer name
  (c) customer date of birth
  (d) customer telephone number (1 mark)

4 Which of the following is used to hold data in a database?
  (a) table
  (b) form
  (c) report
  (d) query (1 mark)

5 In a database system, which two facilities allow some of the data to be selected for output?
  (a) queries and forms
  (b) reports and forms
  (c) queries and reports
  (d) forms and macros (1 mark)

Score /5

B

Answer all parts of all questions.

1 Explain the difference between a database and a management system.

....

.... (2 marks)

2 State three functions that can be carried out by a database report.

....

.... (3 marks)

3 State four design tasks when setting up a database system.

....

.... (4 marks)

4 Explain the difference between a field and a record.

....

.... (2 marks)

5 Explain why someone might set up a query when using a database.

....

.... (2 marks)

Score /13

These are GCSE style questions. Answer all parts of the questions.

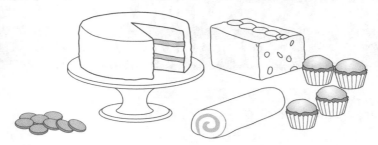

1 The table shows part of a database used by a bakery shop. It is called the **Stock_table**.

Item_number	Item_name	Category	Weight	Selling_Price
A1453	ginger cake	cake	500	1.5
B6453	chocolate muffin	cake	150	0.4
C5645	egg custard	pastry	150	0.45

(a) How many records are shown?

.... (1 mark)

(b) How many fields are shown?

.... (1 mark)

(c) The manager of the shop wants a printout of the names of all the items in the cake category, showing their selling prices. Explain, as a series of steps, what the software would have to do in order to produce this list.

....

....

....

.... (6 marks)

(d) State which field in this table would be used as a **key field** and explain your reasons.

....

.... (2 marks)

(e) State which data type would be suitable to store the **Item_number** data and explain your reasons.

....

.... (2 marks)

Score   /12

TOTAL SCORE   /30

For more on this topic
see pages 30–31 of your Success Guide

COMMON APPLICATIONS – DATABASE MANAGEMENT SOFTWARE

A   Choose just one answer, a, b, c or d.

1 A database report can be used
(a) to store data
(b) to provide a user interface
(c) to group data
(d) to update data.   (1 mark)

2 Which of the following could be a database form control?
(a) a field
(b) a record
(c) a table
(d) a command button   (1 mark)

3 Which of the following is a type of software?
(a) database
(b) field
(c) database management system
(d) file   (1 mark)

4 A car owner regularly takes his car to the same dealer for servicing. The details of the job are stored in a service table. The best choice of a key field for this table is
(a) job number
(b) car registration number
(c) customer number
(d) date of service.   (1 mark)

5 On a database form, objects can be placed to collect and display data. These objects are called
(a) labels
(b) records
(c) controls
(d) tables.   (1 mark)

Score   /5

B   Answer all parts of all questions.

1 Fill in the blanks.

When users choose different options from their database software, they use a .... If they want printed output from the database, they generate a .... Data is input into the database using a screen .... which may have .... These allow many screens to be available by using button clicks. When choices have to be made between a limited set of options, the screen will have .... on it.   (5 marks)

2 A database system is used to handle a company's payroll operations.

(a) State three different data tables that may be required.

....

....

....   (3 marks)

(b) For any one of these tables, describe a situation where data may need to be

(i) added ....

(ii) altered ....

(iii) deleted ....   (3 marks)

Score   /11

This is a GCSE style question. Answer all parts of the question.

1 Nina runs a small music school. Part of her business involves organising instrumental and singing lessons for customers. She has a number of music teachers on her books. She wants a computer system to help her organise the bookings. She has to decide whether to have a computer system specially written or to buy one that already exists 'off the shelf'.

(a) State **three** advantages of buying the software 'off the shelf'.

....

....

.... (3 marks)

(b) State **two** advantages of having the software specially written.

....

.... (2 marks)

(c) On a separate piece of paper, design a screen that could be used to make a lesson booking. (5 marks)

(d) Nina decides to expand her business by selling musical instruments. Describe an extra module she might need to add to her software to help with this.

....

.... (2 marks)

Score   /12

How well did you do?

0–9   Try again
10–14 Getting there
15–23 Good work
24–28 Excellent!

TOTAL SCORE   /28

For more on this topic see pages 32–33 of your Success Guide

COMMON APPLICATIONS – SPREADSHEETS

A

Choose just one answer, a, b, c or d.

1 In a spreadsheet, cell A12 contains the value 6. Cell A13 contains the value 10 cm. The formula =A12*A13 is entered into cell A14 to multiply these values. An error occurs. This is because
(a) the wrong cell references have been used
(b) A13 contains text data
(c) the wrong sign for multiply has been used
(d) A12 contains the wrong type of data.
(1 mark)

2 A graph is required every month to display sales figures. The same process is always used. Which is the most efficient way of doing this?
(a) a macro   (c) a formula
(b) a wizard   (d) select chart from menu
(1 mark)

3 In a spreadsheet, cell A1 contains the value 4, A2 contains 5 and A3 contains 6. Cell A4 contains the expression =(A1+A2)*A3. What would be displayed in cell A4?

(a) 34   (b) 1.5   (c) 24   (d) 54
(1 mark)

4 In a spreadsheet, cell C12 contains the value 6. D12 contains the value 12 and D14, the value 10. Cell E16 contains the expression =C12*(D12–D14). What is the value displayed in cell E16?
(a) –12   (b) 12   (c) 62   (d) 8   (1 mark)

5 A spreadsheet program can be used to construct a simple database. Which of these database actions can be performed by a spreadsheet?
(a) link tables   (c) sort data
(b) use queries   (d) produce reports
(1 mark)

Score   /5

B

Answer all parts of all questions.

1 Use the following words to fill in the gaps.

row	column	model	cell	address

Spreadsheet software holds data in boxes, each of which is called a .... Each of these has a unique .... , which is referenced by a vertical .... and a horizontal .... Spreadsheets can be used to set up mathematical relationships which together can .... a real-life scenario. (5 marks)

2 Spreadsheets allow users to produce macros.

(a) Explain what a macro is.

.... (2 marks)

(b) Describe one suitable use for a macro.

.... (2 marks)

(c) Explain how macros can be helpful to a user.

.... (2 marks)

3 Explain what is meant by a spreadsheet formula.

.... (3 marks)

Score   /14

C These are GCSE style questions. Answer all parts of the questions.

1 This table shows how sales of revision books are expected to increase each month. The actual sales figures for January are entered and then it is assumed that sales will increase by 10 per cent each month from January to June.

	A	B	C	D	E	F	G	H
1	Revision Books Monthly Sales							
2								
3		Jan	Feb	Mar	Apr	May	Jun	Totals
4	English	1,000	1,100	1,210	1,331	1,464	1,611	7,716
5	French	1,324	1,456	1,602	1,762	1,938	2,132	10,215
6	History	897	987	1,085	1,194	1,313	1,445	6,921
7	ICT	1,432	1,575	1,733	1,906	2,097	2,306	11,049
8	Maths	1,213	1,334	1,468	1,615	1,776	1,954	9,359
9	Science	906	997	1,096	1,206	1,326	1,459	6,990
10	**Total**	**6,772**	**7,449**	**8,194**	**9,014**	**9,914**	**10,907**	**52,250**

(a) Identify the formula that would be placed in cell C4.

.... (2 marks)

(b) Identify the formula that would be placed in cell D4.

.... (2 marks)

(c) It is found that the January sales figure for English books was entered incorrectly. The figure should have been 900. The correct figure is entered. The correct new figure for February's estimate is calculated by hand to check that it is calculated correctly. State what this figure should be.

.... (1 mark)

(d) State the cell address of any cell that would contain a function.

.... (1 mark)

(e) State in detail, the contents of cell H9.

.... (3 marks)

(f) The publisher of the books wants to produce a chart to show how the sales of each title in January compare with each other. Briefly explain how this could be done.

....

.... (2 marks)

Score   /11

How well did you do?

0–10   Try again
11–15   Getting there
16–25   Good work
26–30   Excellent!

TOTAL SCORE   /30

**For more on this topic
see pages 34–35 of your Success Guide**

COMMON APPLICATIONS – DTP AND GRAPHICS

A

Choose just one answer, a, b, c or d.

1 Which software would be best for setting out a complex page, with text and graphics?
(a) desktop publisher
(b) word processor
(c) graphics software
(d) computer-aided design software (1 mark)

2 One disadvantage of bit-mapped graphics is
(a) the file cannot be compressed
(b) colours are not represented accurately
(c) few applications can display them
(d) the image becomes jagged when rescaled. (1 mark)

3 Vector graphics methods store pictures by
(a) storing the details of every pixel
(b) using mathematical expressions
(c) compressing the image details
(d) embedding the details in a document. (1 mark)

4 Software that is used to help in the design of engineering components is called
(a) CAM   (c) CAD
(b) CAL   (d) CAT. (1 mark)

5 Which of these is an advantage of vector graphics?
(a) the files do not take up much disk space
(b) the image quality is always good
(c) the image can be rescaled smoothly
(d) the file can be imported into many applications. (1 mark)

Score   /5

B

Answer all parts of all questions.

1 List three ways that images may be produced for use in a desktop publishing document.

....

.... (3 marks)

2 Describe three ways in which an image can be manipulated by CAD software.

....

.... (3 marks)

3 (a) Explain what is meant by bit-mapped graphic files.

....

.... (2 marks)

(b) What are two disadvantages of using bit-mapped graphics.

....

.... (2 marks)

(c) Explain how a bit-mapped image can be prepared so that it can be transmitted efficiently over the Internet.

....

.... (3 marks)

Score   /13

These are GCSE style questions. Answer all parts of the questions.

1 A computer superstore is putting together a leaflet advertising its special offers. The leaflet is to be inserted between the pages of the local newspaper.

(a) Explain how they would use word processing and desktop publishing software in producing this leaflet.

....

....

....

....

(4 marks)

The PC Place

**This month's special offers
Starting 1st July
Hundreds of bargains inside**

(b) State, with reasons, **two** other software packages that they might need to produce the leaflet.

....

.... (4 marks)

2 Stephanie is a kitchen designer. She uses a computer to plan kitchen layouts for customers. The software she uses can make use of an extensive data library.

(a) What software would be suitable for producing the plans?

.... (1 mark)

(b) Explain what would be stored in the data library and how this library would help in the design process.

.... (2 marks)

(c) Stephanie needs to produce large diagrams of the plans on paper for the fitters to use. What output device would be most suitable?

.... (1 mark)

Score   /12

How well did you do?

0–10	Try again
11–15	Getting there
16–25	Good work
26–30	Excellent!

TOTAL SCORE   /30

**For more on this topic
see pages 36–37 of your Success Guide**

MODELS AND SIMULATIONS

A

Choose just one answer, a, b, c or d.

1 A computer model is
(a) a set of mathematical rules
(b) an output which predicts an event
(c) a computer game
(d) virtual reality. (1 mark)

2 A biologist uses a computer to model the growth of an insect population. The main advantage of using computer modelling in this case is
(a) the results are likely to be very accurate
(b) there are very few variables to take into account
(c) more generations can be tested in a limited time
(d) the results will always be the same. (1 mark)

3 A computer game allows the player to simulate driving cars around city streets. Which of these is an input into the system?
(a) the detection of a crash
(b) movement of a paddle on the console
(c) the car engine sound
(d) arrival at a cross-road (1 mark)

4 Flight simulators are used to train pilots. One reason for doing this is because
(a) flight simulators are more realistic than flying an actual plane
(b) situations can be modelled that are rare in real-life
(c) the modelled plane behaves more unpredictably
(d) it is easier to fly a 'virtual' plane. (1 mark)

5 Computer simulations are sometimes used to predict the performance of a real-life situation, such as the crash behaviour of cars. One reason for using computers in this way is
(a) computer-generated results are likely to be more reliable
(b) you can be sure that all relevant factors are taken into account
(c) more variables can be investigated at the same time
(d) much greater precision is possible. (1 mark)

Score /5

B

Answer all parts of all questions.

1 Fill in the gaps.

Many computer games allow the player to experience an imaginary place. This is called .... Some games have very realistic graphics and sound. They require the computer to have a very fast .... so that the action is smooth. To hold all the graphic data, the computer also needs a great deal of .... (3 marks)

2 Explain why predictions made from computer models may not always be reliable.

....

.... (2 marks)

3 Explain the relationship between a model and a simulation.

....

....

.... (3 marks)

Score /8

C These are GCSE style questions. Answer all parts of the questions.

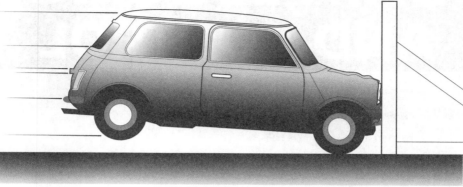

1 A car manufacturer wants to test how safe a new model is when it is involved in a collision. A computer is used to model the situation.

(a) Explain **two** reasons why computer modelling is an advantage in this case.

....

.... (4 marks)

(b) Describe **two** items of data that would be needed to allow the model to work properly.

....

.... (4 marks)

(c) Explain why the manufacturer still has to carry out some real crash tests.

....

.... (3 marks)

2 Weather forecasting makes use of modelling techniques. State **two** items of data that would be used by the software.

....

.... (2 marks)

3 When planning a country's budget, civil servants have to make use of economic models, which are implemented on a computer.

(a) Explain what is meant by an economic model.

....

.... (2 marks)

(b) State **two** items of data that could usefully be fed into such a model.

....

.... (2 marks)

Score   /17

How well did you do?

0–10   Try again
11–15   Getting there
16–25   Good work
26–30   Excellent!

TOTAL SCORE   /30

**For more on this topic
see pages 38–39 of your Success Guide**

DATA LOGGING AND CONTROL

A   Choose just one answer, a, b, c or d.

1 When data is being logged by computer, the input device is
(a) a sensor
(b) an analogue/digital converter
(c) an interface
(d) an actuator. (1 mark)

2 A small computer is used in a car to show how far the driver can expect to go before needing to refuel. This type of computer system is called
(a) process control   (c) an embedded system
(b) a simulation   (d) interactive. (1 mark)

3 A computer is used to make sure that the products from an oil refinery are consistent. This application of computers is called
(a) simulation
(b) process control
(c) modelling
(d) data logging. (1 mark)

4 Which of these is an example of computer control?
(a) weather forecasting
(b) economic modelling
(c) robotics
(d) data logging (1 mark)

5 A computer-controlled greenhouse is set to turn the heater on if it gets too cold and turn it off if it gets too hot. A system like this where output affects the next input makes use of
(a) feedback
(b) batch processing
(c) multiprogramming
(d) OMR. (1 mark)

Score /5

B   Answer all parts of all questions.

1 Fill in the gaps.

When a computer system is logging data, it needs input from a .... These devices usually produce a varying voltage, which is known as an .... signal. The computer needs to receive .... signals, so an .... converter is usually required. When temperature data is being sampled, a .... is used to detect the temperature changes.
(5 marks)

2 Give three reasons why computer data logging has advantages over humans taking measurements.

....

.... (3 marks)

3 When collecting data by automatic data logging, it is important to sample data at sensible intervals. Fill in the following table with the appropriate letter to suggest suitable time intervals, taken from this list:

A every microsecond	B every minute	C every week

Situation	Sampling interval
Temperature changes during an explosion	
Temperature data to investigate global warming	
The cooling of a cup of coffee	

(3 marks)
Score /11

C These are GCSE style questions. Answer all parts of the questions.

1 A robot has been programmed to tidy up a room. It is able to respond only to these instructions:

Instruction	Meaning
FD (n)	Forward (number of squares) in the direction its head is pointing
RT (n)	Turn right (number of degrees)
LT (n)	Turn left (number of degrees)
GRAB	Grab whatever is in the square
DROP	Drop whatever it is holding

(a) Write a series of instructions that will cause the robot to put the drink can in the bin. You should use as few instructions as you can.

....

.... **(5 marks)**

(b) The robot makers add a new capability to the robot's instruction set. It is REPEAT (n)... END REPEAT. This means repeat (number of times) all the actions given until the END REPEAT instruction. For example,

```
REPEAT (4)
FD (2)
RT (90)
END REPEAT
```
makes the robot move round in a square.

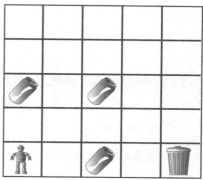

Use the REPEAT feature and whatever other instructions are necessary, to program the robot to clear away these three drinks cans to the bin.

....

.... **(4 marks)**

2 A burglar alarm system has two sensors, a pressure pad and an infrared detector. It has to be armed before it can be activated by an intruder. It has one output device – an alarm. In the table below, 0 means 'No' and 1 means 'Yes'. For each of the circumstances in the table, indicate whether the alarm is on or off by using 0 or 1. **(3 marks)**

Armed	Pressure Pad	Infrared detector	Alarm
1	0	1	
1	0	0	
0	1	0	

Score /12

How well did you do?

0–9	Try again
10–14	Getting there
15–23	Good work
24–28	Excellent!

TOTAL SCORE   /28

For more on this topic see pages 40–41 of your Success Guide

TABLES, FIELDS AND RECORDS

A Choose just one answer, a, b, c or d.

1 A video store has a collection of DVDs that it hires out to customers. Information about the DVDs is held on a database. In this case, a DVD is
(a) an entity   (c) a field
(b) a file   (d) a record.   (1 mark)

2 A data field is required to store a telephone number in the form 0121-444 1234. The data type required would be
(a) double   (c) text
(b) integer   (d) number.   (1 mark)

3 Often, data is stored in a database in coded form. An advantage of this is
(a) hackers won't be able to understand it
(b) it is easier for the software to sort the data
(c) it doesn't need validating
(d) it takes less storage space.   (1 mark)

4 Why is it a mistake to use a text data type to store money values?
(a) the pound or dollar sign cannot be displayed
(b) the decimal point cannot be displayed
(c) calculations cannot be performed
(d) the data cannot be sorted   (1 mark)

5 In a database about school pupils, one field records whether a pupil has had a TB vaccination. The most efficient data type to store this fact will be
(a) text   (c) number
(b) boolean   (d) memo.   (1 mark)

Score   /5

B Answer all parts of all questions.

1 Fill in the blanks.

Something you store data about is called an .... All the data about one of these makes

up a .... and it is stored, together with others, in a .... One item of

data is called a .... and if this is used to provide a unique identity, it is called a

....   (5 marks)

2 Identify the data types that would be used for the following:

(a) a telephone number such as 01808 715248 ....

(b) a forename such as Jason ....

(c) a postcode such as E19 4RD ....

(d) whether someone has paid a bill or not ....

(e) the total amount of a bill such as £4.50. ....

     (5 marks)

3 Explain why data often needs to be encoded when entered into a database.

....

....   (3 marks)

Score   /13

C These are GCSE style questions. Answer all parts of the questions.

1 An electrical store needs to keep data about its products in a relational database. One of the tables is called STOCK. Its structure is as follows:

Field name	Field type	Field Size	Example
Stock_Number	Number	4 bytes	345
Item_Name	Text	15 bytes	Breadmaker
Supplier_Code	Text	6 bytes	AB786
Selling_Price	Currency	8 bytes	120.00
Number_in_Stock	Number	4 bytes	20
Date_last_ordered	Date	8 bytes	12/02/03

(a) The store currently has 500 products in stock. Calculate the minimum file size required to store all the necessary data. Show how you work this out.

....

....

....

(3 marks)

(b) Which field would be suitable for a key field and explain why.

....

.... (2 marks)

(c) The store needs to be able to telephone its suppliers when enquiring about orders. Explain how the data about the suppliers, such as the telephone number, would be stored in an effective way.

....

.... (3 marks)

2 (a) Explain what is meant by a **fixed length** field.

....

.... (2 marks)

(b) Give **two** reasons why fixed length fields can be an advantage in a database.

....

.... (2 marks)

Score   /12

How well did you do?

0–10   Try again
11–15 Getting there
16–25 Good work
26–30 Excellent!

TOTAL SCORE   /30

For more on this topic
see pages 44–45 of your Success Guide

DATA CAPTURE

A

Choose just one answer, a, b, c or d.

1 A form control that gives a drop down box with the allowable choices displayed is called
(a) a check box   (c) a menu
(b) a list box   (d) a text box.   (1 mark)

2 Which screen object can be used to select one option from a series of valid responses?
(a) radio button
(b) text box
(c) command button
(d) data object   (1 mark)

3 Sometimes when data is entered into a computer system, it is typed in twice by two different operators. This is an example of
(a) validation
(b) data backup

(c) data redundancy
(d) verification.   (1 mark)

4 A database system allows users to pick a data item from a list when entering data. This is best achieved by using which screen control?
(a) a text box
(b) a button
(c) a combo box
(d) a menu   (1 mark)

5 Verification means
(a) checking that input data is reasonable
(b) checking that input data is accurate
(c) checking that output data is reasonable
(d) checking that output data is correct.
                   (1 mark)

Score   /5

B

Answer all parts of all questions.

1 Fill in the blanks.

Verification is used to check that data is .... It can be carried out by .... operators entering the same data. The two versions are .... by the computer which reports on any ....   (4 marks)

2 State four characteristics of a well-designed data capture form.

....

.... (4 marks)

3 Explain what is meant by batch processing.

....

.... (4 marks)

Score   /12

C These are GCSE style questions. Answer all parts of the questions.

1 ABC Computers Ltd has a team of sales people. They travel all over the country, trying to get new orders and helping existing customers. They spend money on many things while they are travelling, such as petrol, train fares, hotels, meals and telephone calls. Every week they fill in an expenses claim form to get back the money that they have spent.

On a separate piece of paper, design an expenses claim form for ABC Computers Ltd. It must be easy and quick to fill in. (6 marks)

2 Regal Video Store has a computer-based system for keeping stock records. This is the data entry screen that is used to enter data about new videos when they are delivered.

(a) Identify **one** data item where data entry could be confusing for the operator. Explain how the data entry screen could be improved in this case.

....

....

.... (2 marks)

(b) One field, **Entered by**, is for the operator's name. Explain how, in this case, the likelihood of error is reduced.

....

.... (2 marks)

(c) Explain how the entry of the **category** data helps to reduce error.

....

.... (3 marks)

3 Much of the data intended for computer systems is still captured on paper forms.

(a) Explain why paper forms are a popular method of data capture.

....

.... (2 marks)

(b) Explain why paper forms can often lead to error in the capture of data.

....

.... (2 marks)

Score   /17

How well did you do?
0–11 Try again
12–17 Getting there
18–29 Good work
30–34 Excellent!

TOTAL SCORE   /34

For more on this topic see pages 46–47 of your Success Guide

VALIDATION

A Choose just one answer, a, b, c or d.

1 A postcode such as W4 5TF is stored in a database field. The data type needed is
(a) number (c) text
(b) memo (d) boolean. (1 mark)

2 A database system allows users to pick a data item from a list when entering data. This is best achieved by using which screen control?
(a) a text box (c) a menu
(b) a button (d) a combo box (1 mark)

3 Modulus 11 is a common method of determining
(a) a hash total
(b) a check digit
(c) parity
(d) that data is the correct type. (1 mark)

4 A database system is used to store details of job applicants. It is designed to reject any dates of birth for people too young or too old. The validation check in this case is
(a) a range check
(b) a length check
(c) a type check
(d) a check digit. (1 mark)

5 A person's name is a file in a database. The software prevents the operator accidentally typing in numbers. This form of check is called
(a) a type check
(b) a range check
(c) a check digit
(d) a presence check. (1 mark)

Score /5

B Answer all parts of all questions.

1 Fill in the blanks.

Validation is carried out by the .... on data when it is being ....

It makes sure that the data is .... (3 marks)

2 British car registration plates are now of the form LLNNLLL, where L = letter and N = number. The numbers are based on the half year period when registered, for example 02 means the first half of 2002, 52 means the second half. Here are some registrations of cars to be sold. They were typed in by an operator in March 2003. For each one, say whether it is valid. If not, describe and explain the validation check that would prevent it from being accepted.

(a) VX52CXZ ....

(b) VXC52XY.............................

(c) VX53CDE.............................

(d) VX03CXZA............................. (10 marks)

Score /13

46

These are GCSE style questions. Answer all parts of the questions.

1 Cunningham Library has a computerised system to deal with the issue and return of books. When somebody wants to become a member of the library, a form has to be filled in. On the form, the applicant has to provide a name, date of birth, telephone number, house number and postcode.

For each of these **five** items of data, describe a suitable validation check that would need to be performed. (5 marks)

Data item	Validation check
Name	
Date of birth	
Telephone number	
House number	
Postcode	

2 Vinnie is the librarian on duty. A borrower wants to take out a book. He gives the book and his library card to Vinnie.

Vinnie scans the bar code in the book and another on the library card. When the library card is scanned, the computer performs a check digit validation check on the number.

CUNNINGHAM LIBRARY
44-46 Tower Road
West Green
Cunningham

Name.....*Bob Smith*...........

No.....07736.........

(a) What data will be encoded in the bar-code of the library card?

.... (1 mark)

(b) Explain the purpose of the **check digit**.

.... (1 mark)

(c) Explain how a **check digit** is produced.

....

.... (3 marks)

(d) Explain why the bar-coded number is also printed on the card in ordinary numbers.

.... (2 marks)

Score   /12

How well did you do?

0–10	Try again
11–15	Getting there
16–25	Good work
26–30	Excellent!

TOTAL SCORE   /30

For more on this topic see pages 48–49 of your Success Guide

DATA CAPTURE AND VALIDATION

A **Choose just one answer, a, b, c or d.**

1 Validation is carried out when data is
(a) input   (c) processed
(b) stored   (d) output.   (1 mark)

2 Often data is stored in a database in coded form. An advantage of this is
(a) hackers won't be able to understand it
(b) it is easier for the software to sort the data
(c) it takes up less storage space
(d) it doesn't need validating.   (1 mark)

3 Validation ensures that
(a) data are accurate
(b) data are up to date
(c) data are secure
(d) data are reasonable.   (1 mark)

4 Why is it a mistake to use a text data type to store money values?
(a) the pound or dollar sign cannot be displayed
(b) the decimal point cannot be displayed
(c) the data cannot be sorted
(d) calculations cannot be performed   (1 mark)

5 A car registration must now be in the format of letter, letter, number, number, letter, letter, letter. To ensure that this arrangement is correct when data are entered into a database, which check would be used?
(a) a range check   (c) a check digit
(b) a picture check   (d) a presence check.
     (1 mark)

Score   /5

B **Answer all parts of all questions.**

1 (a) Describe what is meant by a batch process.

....

.... (2 marks)

(b) Describe two characteristics of a process that make it suitable for batch processing.

....

.... (2 marks)

(c) State two examples of situations where batch processing is suitable.

....

.... (2 marks)

2 Describe two ways in which a data capture form can help the person filling it in to provide the right information.

....

.... (4 marks)

3 An Internet e-mail service provides an on-screen form to apply for an e-mail address. State any one field that would be compulsory for the applicant to fill in.

.... (1 mark)

Score   /11

Letts

NEW

GCSE

SUCCESS

VISUAL
REVISION
GUIDE

QUESTIONS & ANSWERS

ICT

Sean O'Byrne

ANSWER BOOK

COMPUTER SYSTEMS

Section A
1 c 3 b 5 b
2 d 4 a

Section B
1 data, programmed, mainframes, network
2 (a) A = input, B = process, C = output, D = storage
  (b)

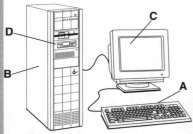

Section C
1 (a) physical devices, any reasonable choice such as any peripheral or internal or network physical component.
  (b) programs/instructions, that tell the computer what to do, plus documentation (any two of these points)
2 data can be sent to it/stored in it, and data can be retrieved from it, by the processor (any three points – no marks for repeating the words 'read' or 'write')
3 (a) Random Access Memory, volatile/data lost when power is off, stores user's programs and data, any part can be accessed directly by the processor, large amounts of RAM compared to ROM (any five points)
  (b) start-up/boot routines, input/output routines (any one point)
4

Hardware	Software
RAM	Windows
Network interface card	Payroll processing system
Hard disk controller	Printer driver
Processor	Word processor

INPUT AND OUTPUT

Section A
1 d 3 a 5 c
2 b 4 b

Section B
1 (a) MICR – prevents fraudulent entries/human and machine readable
  (b) magnetic strip – encodes small amount of identity data/can be read quickly by machine
  (c) bar-code – encodes item identity/read quickly by scanners/allows itemised bills/relatively cheap equipment needed to read
  (d) OMR – easy to encode/only needs pencil to encode, quickly read by machine (four identifications plus four comments)

---

2 scan image, scan document, digitise image, OCR software needed to convert, image file to text file (any three points)

Section C
1 printer for permanent copy/for handing work in, modem for Internet access/e-mails, floppy drive for backups/to take work away, CD drive for archiving/multimedia data sources/music, scanner for digitising pictures
2 laser for leaflets – gives high quality, dot matrix for bills – can produce carbon copies as impact printer
3 concept keyboard – choose food items from pictures, no need for typing, card reader – to read data from credit/debit cards, thermal or dot matrix printer – to produce bills, screen – to display choices/bills

STORAGE DEVICES AND MEDIA

Section A
1 b 3 d 5 a
2 c 4 d

Section B
1 backup, to take files away, transfer to another computer
2 a group of tracks, on separate disk surfaces, all at the same position (any two points)
3 (a) tracks
  (b) sector

Section C
1 (a) inscribe magnetic tracks, divide into sectors, produce filing system
  (b) floppy disk only holds 1.44 MB, pictures can be very large, probable that document is therefore too big to fit on floppy
2 (a) (hard) disk
  (b) immediate response/update required, this needs random access files, only possible on disk
3 light, portable, large capacity, robust, rapid reading, software tends to be large files (any three points)

THE CPU

Section A
1 c 3 b 5 b
2 c 4 d

Section B
1 (a) processor, (memory) location, silicon
  (b) disk, RAM/memory, processor, decoded, executed/carried out
2 allows processor to make decisions, carry out instructions, perform arithmetic, make decisions (any two points)
3 faster clock speed – the more instructions can be processed per second/in a given time, therefore faster running of program
4 (a) Y
  (b) N
  (c) Y
  (d) N

Section C
1 (a) no action
  (b) drain valve opens and pump started
  (c) no action
  (d) no action
2 c, e, a, d, b

BITS AND BYTES

Section A
1 a 3 d 5 b
2 c 4 c

Section B
1 (a) American Standard Code for Information Interchange, numbers/bits, Unicode/EBCDIC
  (b) bit, BInary digiT, byte
2 binary
3 instructions, numbers, characters, sounds, pictures, etc
4 the location gives the meaning

Section C
1 (a) 262,144 K
  (b) operating system, applications, data, output data, input data (any four points)
  (c) pictures are made of pixels, which are small dots, many are needed to make up a picture, this takes a lot of storage
  (d) CD writer (rewriter) used to copy files onto CD, CD useful to store files for transport to a different location, or for backup, moving images take a lot of storage space, CD required to have sufficient capacity (any three points)
2 BYTE
3 switch can be on or off, switch state can represent data such as 0/1, true/false

NETWORKS

Section A
1 a 3 b 5 c
2 c 4 b

Section B
1 (a) LAN: confined to one site, WAN: spread over wide geographical area
  (b) LAN: cable/radio, WAN: telephone, ISDN, leased lines, satellite links (any three points)
  (c) (i) LAN
    (ii) fibre-optic, little signal loss over long distances, great band width/carries many signals at once, less affected by weather/deterioration issues (any three points)
2 server/file server

Section C
1 (a) work from different rooms, backup easier, central storage of data, shared peripherals (any three points)
  (b) time taken to set up, expense of hardware, expense of network operating system, expertise required to set up, possibility of virus spreading throughout network (any three points)

  (c) network interface card (NIC) – to connect computers to network, cable – to link computers together, hub/switch – to link more than one computer to server
  (d) connects to telephone system, converts analogue to digital signals, and vice versa, computer uses digital signals, telephone system uses analogue signals (any three points)
  (e) faster transmission/greater bandwidth, carries digital signals, so no need to convert using a modem
2 (a) easier to organise with separation of functions, e-mail server/web server for processing on-line orders, file server for storage of shared files and software, printer resources, backup in case there are problems with one (any three points)
  (b) backup copies on two servers, password protection, restricted access to files and directories/folders, different permissions granted to different people (any two points)
  (c) (i) need for expertise to run network/other staff do not have time to run network
    (ii) network manager/ systems manager, to oversee network/make decisions/arrange maintenance, etc

    or

    technician or suitable description, to see to routine tasks such as backups/addition/ maintenance of user accounts, etc (two marks, one for job title/ description, one for suitable duty performed)

NETWORKS – LAYOUTS AND SOFTWARE

Section A
1 a 3 d 5 b
2 b 4 a

Section B
1 (a) bus network
  (b) A = terminator, B = workstation/client, C = (bus) cable, D = server
  (c) cheap, easy to install (any one point)
  (d) many data collisions, can be slow, if there is a cabling fault the whole network is affected (any two points)

Section C
1 no server, all workstations 'equal', one may be chosen to store the files
2 cheap to install, not many users, so unlikely to be data traffic problems
3 (a) more than one process executed (apparently) simultaneously, processor divides its time between processes

(b) requests from different workstations need to be processed, without delaying users

(c) software stored in one location is easier to upgrade; better network performance as one machine specialises in network administrative functions/not dividing its time between networking and acting as workstation; central storage of data makes group working easier

4 provision of groups, provision of rights, arranged for each group/individual, protection against software deletion, read-only files, activity logs, password checking, other reasonable points (any three points)

5 establishes the identity of the user, gives access to appropriate network resources, connects with server (any two points)

COMMUNICATION METHODS

Section A
1 c 3 a 5 b
2 b 4 d

Section B
1 (a) quick delivery, file attachments, cheap, automatic record keeping, can pick up anywhere, reliable, can be sent any time (any four points)

   (b) can be insecure, computer resources required, junk mail/spam, virus risk, can be misinterpreted as often brief, easily passed around

2 advertising, collecting orders, providing after sales support, collecting market research data, collecting customer details (any three points)

3 large amounts of data transmitted, because many pictures involved, many frames per second, to produce smooth movement, broadband can send lots of data per second, 10 MB plus (any four points)

Section C
Suitable method of communication – any one point for each box; reason – any one point for each box.

1 **Sending a message to his son:** mobile phone;   text message short, can be picked up as convenient/time differences, cheap to send

   Discussing a customer's account with the sales manager: telephone; immediate, can exchange ideas live, tone of voice helps

   Demonstrating a product to a number of customers in different locations: video conferencing; can display product, immediate

   Send a spreadsheet file to head office: e-mail; fast to deliver, can send as attachment, recipient can work with the file

2 broadband/lots of data sent in

given time, useful for television services, digital is such good quality, no need to connect to land lines

DATA TRANSFER

Section A
1 a 3 d 5 d
2 b 4 c

Section B
1 (a) data takes less space, reduces download/transmission times

   (b)
Standard	Type of file
jpeg	image
gif	image
mpeg	moving picture

2 many users have modems, modems have slow download speeds, often no more than 128 Kbps, graphics are often large files, hence page loads slowly (any four points)

3 (a) 1 MB = 1,024 x 1,024 x 8bits
   1 MB = 8,388, 608 bits
   56 Kbps = 56,000 bits per second,
   Time taken = 8,388,608 /56,000 seconds
   = 149.8 seconds
   = 2.5 minutes

   (b) phone line/ISP may be slower, bottlenecks, part of the line may be sharing with other transmissions (any two points)

Section C
1 (a) bus cable may be subject to many data collisions, replace with star or ring topology

   (b) network cards may have low maximum speed, replace cards

   (c) server may have insufficient RAM/old hard disk specification, add more RAM/replace hard disk/add new hard disk drive

2 less data travelling over network cables, therefore fewer collisions

3 large amounts of RAM, fast processors, fast/large disk drives, because many users accessing servers simultaneously, high specification allows more effective multitasking (any three points)

OPERATING SYSTEMS 1

Section A
1 b 3 d 5 a
2 c 4 c

Section B
1 Application: A, D, E, F
   Operating system: B, C

2 disk, RAM/memory, booting, hardware

3 different programs stored in RAM, processor divides attention between them, allocates each a 'time slice'

Section C
1 (a) connect to network/server, establish identity, establish rights/privileges (any two

points)

   (b) printer, scanner, disk drive, data, (any) software, Internet connection (any two points)

2 (a) container/folder, to keep files in

   (b) one directory contains other directories, all descend from root

3 (a) allows immediate response, to input or output is quick enough, to influence next input (any two points)

   (b) computer game, flight control, process control, traffic lights (or any other situation where immediate response is needed)

   (c) rapid response necessary, to allow system to keep pace with events

OPERATING SYSTEMS 2

Section A
1 b 3 a 5 c
2 d 4 b

Section B
1 (a) types commands, at a prompt, computer translates commands

   (b) can batch commands together, fast response, uses little RAM

2 delete, rename, move, copy

3 (a) position mouse over object, press mouse button, used for selection

   (b) hold mouse button down, while moving mouse, for moving objects

Section C
1 (a) means of interacting with computer, allows input, and output (any two points)

   (b) windows, (drop-down/pop-up) menus, dialogue boxes, buttons, combo boxes, scroll bars, etc

   (c) easy to use/intuitive, no need to learn commands

2 extra RAM: to allow for increased storage, because GUIs are bit-mapped, therefore large files (any two points)
   Faster processor: screen needs refreshing/redrawing often, greater complexity of the software.

3 (a) dialogue box

   (b) allows several items to be set, then all accepted at once, related commands grouped together, for ease of understanding (any two points)

COMMON APPLICATIONS – WORD PROCESSING

Section A
1 b 3 d 5 a
2 c 4 c

Section B
1 (a) general purpose software, can be customised to suit user.

(b)
Generic	Special purpose
Desktop publishing	Traffic light control
Spreadsheet	Automatic camera control
Web browser	Insurance premium calculations

2 examples: proper names, foreign words, technical terms, abbreviations, etc

Section C
1 insertion of variable data, into a standard document, use of fields, need data source (any three points).

2 The order is as follows:

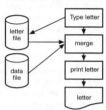

3 These are example answers – many others may be possible; word processing for writing letters, spreadsheet for accounts/invoices, database software for stock/customer records, web browser to access Internet e-mail software to communicate with customers, graphics, software to design the covers

COMMON APPLICATIONS – DATABASE SOFTWARE

Section A
1 d 3 a 5 c
2 b 4 a

Section B
1 database is the store of data, database management system is the software that handles the data

2 combining data from different tables, printing data, searching for data, placing data in order

3 designing: forms, data tables, relationships, queries, macros, software modules, reports, interfaces (any four points)

4 a field is **one data** item about an entity, a record is **all the data** about **one** entity in a data table

5 to extract a subset of the data/to find particular items of data, to select certain records or fields to link tables together

Section C
1 (a) 3

   (b) 5

   (c) This can be represented as:
   SELECT Item_name, Category, Price FROM Stock-table WHERE Category="cake"
   (marks for the three correct fields, Item_name, Category, Selling-Price, the name of the table, the field with a condition (Category) and the category being looked for (cake)

(d) Item_number, because it uniquely identifies each record

(e) text/string/alphanumeric, because it contains letters

COMMON APPLICATIONS – DATABASE MANAGEMENT SOFTWARE

Section A
1 c 3 c 5 c
2 d 4 a

Section B
1 menu, report, form, tabbed pages, check boxes
2 (a) examples – there will be other valid choices: employee/personnel, hours worked, tax tables, holidays
   (b) examples – there will be many possibilities: (i) new employee hired, (ii) change of address/tax code, (iii) employee leaves

Section C
1 (a) available immediately, should be free of bugs as extensively tested, cheaper, plenty of help available
   (b) specially made to suit her own business, specific training and support available from software provider
   (c) three marks for including relevant fields such as customer details (eg name/address/phone), teacher details (similar), date/time of booking; one mark for heading such as name of company or 'booking details'; one mark for OK/Cancel buttons or some means of confirming or cancelling transaction
   (d) stock control/ordering, to keep details of what/how many of each item is in stock or what has been/needs to be ordered

COMMON APPLICATIONS – SPREADSHEETS

Section A
1 b 3 d 5 c
2 a 4 b

Section B
1 cell, address, column, row, model
2 (a) set of steps/statements, which is stored, can be activated/played back, to automate a task
   (b) there are unlimited examples of their use – one mark for a suitable scenario, such as summarising sales data, one mark for a comment on what needs to be done which involves more than one step and also is not generally available on the menu or toolbar, eg plot a chart from a set of figures
   (c) they avoid the need to carry out many separate actions, they make it easy to produce consistent results
3 a set of cell addresses or data and operators (such as +, - * /), to perform a calculation

Section C
1 (a) =B4*1.1 or = B4/100*110 (one mark for B4, one mark for the rest of the formula)
   (b) = C4*1.1 or = C4/100*110 (one mark for C4, one mark for the rest of the formula)
   (c) 990
   (d) Any cell from B10 to H10 or from H4 to H10
   (e) =SUM(B9:G9) (one mark for SUM, one mark for B9, one mark for G9)
   (f) Highlight cells, from A4 to B9, select chart wizard, insert chart, add (any) labels (any two points)

COMMON APPLICATIONS – DTP AND GRAPHICS

Section A
1 a 3 b 5 c
2 d 4 c

Section B
1 digital camera, scanner, art software, clip art
2 rotate, zoom, transform (or example), fill
3 (a) picture divided into dots, or pixels, each dot stored separately
   (b) very large image files, rescaling not smooth
   (c) compressed, characteristics of pixels stored, plus number of repetitions

Section C
1 (a) word processing to originate/edit the text, desktop publishing to create/amend page layout/import text/graphics
   (b) graphics software – manipulate images, file transfer software – to retrieve images from camera, scanner software – to operate scanner
2 (a) CAD (Computer Aided Design)
   (b) images of components/units, saves the need to redraw each time
   (c) plotter

MODELS AND SIMULATIONS

Section A
1 a 3 b 5 c
2 c 4 b

Section B
1 virtual reality, processor, RAM/memory
2 rules may not be fully understood/implemented, data may be insufficient
3 a model is a set of rules/relationships and data, a simulation is a representation of reality, a simulation can be based on a model

Section C
1 (a) cheaper than real crash – no need to destroy lots of cars, safer than real crash – no risk of injury to test personnel, get results quicker/lots of test in a limited time period – computers produce results quickly (any two situations plus reason)

   (b) speed of car – affects severity of crash – energy involved, mass of car – also affects severity of crash/amount of energy involved, layout – eg engine may protect passenger compartment, materials used – different distorting characteristics/strengths (any two sensible suggestions plus explanation)
   (c) to collect the data for the model, in case the model is inadequate, legal reasons require it (any three points)
2 wind speed/direction, temperature, sunshine, rainfall/other precipitation, etc
3 (a) a set of rules, that is intended to describe economic behaviour (of a country), allows predictions (any two points)
   (b) examples: gross national product, unemployment figures, average wages, interest rates, taxation rates, output rates, borrowing, interest repayments, contingencies (any two points – accept other realistic items)

DATA LOGGING AND CONTROL

Section A
1 a 3 b 5 a
2 c 4 c

Section B
1 sensor, analogue, digital, analogue-digital, thermistor
2 no need for human to do the task, more accurate, long/short periods can be better dealt with, data storage advantages, graph plotting facilities
3 A, C, B

Section C
1 (a) FD (1)
   LT (90)
   FD (4)
   GRAB
   LT (90)
   FD (4)
   LT (90)
   FD (4)
   DROP
This is just one example route. If yours works, award 5 marks, but deduct 1 for each instruction in excess of nine stages.
   (b) REPEAT (3)
   FD (2)
   GRAB
   RT (90)
   END REPEAT
   RT (180) or LT (180)
   FD (2)
   DROP
One mark each for: use of REPEAT, END REPEAT, 3 instructions within REPEAT to END REPEAT, final movement instruction, eg FD (2)

TABLES, FIELDS AND RECORDS

Section A
1 a 3 d 5 b
2 c 4 c

Section B

1 entity, record, table, field, key field
2 (a) text (d) Boolean/yes-no
   (b) text (e) number/currency
   (c) text
3 to save storage space, to reduce data entry time (not 'quicker' on its own), to reduce likelihood of making mistakes

Section C
1 (a) size of one record = 45 bytes, therefore total size is at least 500 x 45, ie 22,500 bytes or 43.9 k (must give units)
   (b) Stock_Number, because it can be a unique value
   (c) supplier details in a separate table, linked to the Stock table, by supplier number
2 (a) field length is always the same, in every record, predetermined (any two points)
   (b) overall size can be predicted, easier for software to process/calculate record position

DATA CAPTURE

Section A
1 b 3 d 5 b
2 a 4 c

Section B
1 correct/accurate, two, compared, discrepancies/differences
2 easy/quick to fill in, provides prompts, collects all the information required, collects information in the form that is needed/promotes gathering of structured information, does not gather irrelevant information (any four points)
3 data gathered together, saved onto disk/tape, processed later, no further human intervention required

Section C
1 An easy to read form is needed. Marks are allocated as follows: name of company, heading: 'Expenses form', space for sales person's name, space for sales person's address, prompt for one of these, space for expense description, space for expense amount, expense categories separately entered, prompt for any expense category, prompt for expense amount, prompt for data, space for date, date formatted, character boxes for name or address (up to six marks)

example of marking:

Date: ☐☐ / ☐☐ / ☐☐

This gets three marks – one for the prompt (Date), one for space provided for date, one for formatted date spaces.
2 (a) date field – not formatted, dd/mm/yy would restrict chances of operator error, playing time – not formatted, boxes for hours/minutes or other restriction would reduce possibility of ambiguous entries
   (b) combo box, choice made, spelling errors unlikely (any two points)

(c) radio buttons/option buttons, selection from list of possibles, only one choice possible, wrong entries unlikely (any three points)

3 (a) cheap to produce, cheap to duplicate, can be administered by non-computer staff, can be filled in without access to a computer/without computer knowledge (any two points)

(b) difficult to specify exactly what information is required, individuals may vary in the way they respond to questions, transcription errors, data entry errors (any two points)

VALIDATION

Section A

1 c 3 b 5 a
2 d 4 a

Section B

1 computer/software, entered, reasonable/legal/within limits

2 (a) valid (one point)

(b) invalid: too many letters in first group, format check would trap this (one point & two points)

(c) invalid: 53 refers to second part of year – not reached yet, range check would trap this (one point & two points)

(d) invalid: too many letters in second group, format check or length check would trap this (one point & two points)

Section C

1

Data item	Validation check
Name	character/type/length/presence
Date of birth	type/format
Telephone number	type (alphabetic /text), length
House number	type (numeric)
Postcode	format/presence

2 (a) membership number

(b) to check that the number is valid/legal/reasonable (not 'correct')

(c) a calculation is performed, on all the digits, to produce an extra digit, which is added on to the number (any three points)

(d) if the code is not read properly, the number is still visible

DATA CAPTURE AND VALIDATION

Section A

1 a 3 d 5 b
2 c 4 d

Section B

1 (a) data collected together, all processed in one go, no further human intervention required

(b) repeating records/all records the same format, all records need processing, all records need the same processing done to them (any two points)

(c) electricity (or other) bills, payroll, cheque processing, exam marks processing, other suitable examples (any two reasonable, but different examples)

2 headings – so that purpose is clear, clear prompts – so answers given in form required, boxes to tick – to reduce risk of errors, layout provided eg dates as dd/mm/yy, character boxes – to prevent too much being entered (any four points)

3 name, e-mail address, password, physical address (or part of), any other reasonable field (any one point)

Section C

1 (a) name of company, heading – purpose of form, space for: surname/forename, address, address split into separate lines, gender, date of birth, length of experience, possession of public service vehicle licence, as tick box or similar, character boxes for text fields (any six points)

(b) verification, type the data in twice, computer compares two versions, flags up errors, operator checks with paper data source (any four points)

(c) length check, not too many characters, type check, no invalid characters, picture/format check, date in right form, range check, date not too old or too recent (any four points)

(d) reference number is valid, range check that it lies between lowest and highest permissible, mileage since last service checked – not too small, date of last service checked – not too recent (any four points)

FILES

Section A

1 c 2 b 3 d
4 d 5 b

Section B

1

situation	serial, sequential or random access	reason
a	a clothes shop records each sale as it is made	serial	unpredictable/chronological order
b	a hotel stores details of its rooms to allow on-line bookings to be made	random access	interactive/fast access required
c	a builder's merchant stores details of all its products	sequential	in order for updating purposes
d	a data-logging system stores details of air temperatures over a period of a month	serial	chronological order
e	a sorted file of library loans is used to update the stock file	sequential	in order for updating purposes

2 Transaction files: a, d
Master file: c

Section C

1 (a) this is an interactive process, details are read and changes are written, data needs to be retrieved quickly, updating needs to be done immediately (four individual points)

(b) (hard) disk drive, only disk drives can support random access files

(c) the number is a key field, it is used to calculate the disk address, the disk drive can retrieve Ian's record from that address

(d) the disk address is calculated, from the key field, by using a hashing algorithm, the record can then be located immediately/very quickly (any two points)

2 (a) start at the beginning, read first record, read next record, repeat until 20th record is read (any three of these points)

(b) start at the beginning, go through file until record found, or one greater than one looked for, then record not found

or

allow three stages of binary search such as access middle record, check if record required, if less, search lower half, else search upper half; until subset=1 (any three points)

FILE PROCESSING

Section A

1 b 3 d 5 c
2 c 4 d

Section B

1 sort registration file, read a record from the student file, read a record from the registration file, compare the key fields, write updated record to new student file

2 sort **current_applications** file, read record from **master_applications** file, read record from **current_applications** file, compare keys, if key from **master_applications**<key from **current_applications**, then write record from **master_applications** to new file, move to next **master_applications** record, else write record from **current_applications** to new file, move to next **current_applications** record, repeat until **current_applications** finished, write any remaining master_applications records to new file. (any eight points from this list)

Section C

1 (a)

(b)

(c) if son file lost/corrupted, can be recreated, from old father (master) file, and transaction file

OUTPUT

Section A

1 c 3 a 5 c
2 c 4 b

Section B

1 c, e, f, g

2 a report can: put data into groups, select data, apply different formats, arrange data in order, combine data from different tables, produce summaries

3 (a) printed, output

(b) to take away, as backup, as proof/permanent record (any two points)

(c) output is moving, sound required, interactivity is needed, permanent record not required/save paper, etc

Section C

1 (a) enquiry space, enquiry prompt, 'Go' button or equivalent, area for/example of list of DVDs, indication of hyperlink to further detail, check box or equivalent to mark for order/add to shopping basket, heading to indicate purpose of page (any six points)

(b) (i) search box/sales selection check box or

equivalent/hyperlink
(ii) list of DVDs
(iii) headings/prompts
(c) sound, moving pictures, to allow extracts from DVDs to be experienced
2 (a) serif letters have tags, sans-serif letters do not
(b) quick to understand, show trends

SECURITY

Section A
1 a 3 b 5 c
2 c 4 b

Section B
1 hardware error such as disk drive crash, operator error, power failure during save, other disaster such as fire, software error
2 password, read, encrypted, firewalls, (activity) log
3 security guards, locked rooms, smart cards, stand-alone machines, alarms, bolt down computers, access codes, etc
4 store them off-site, so that if a disaster happens, the data is somewhere else

Section C
1 (a) unauthorised access, to a computer file
(b) explain that credit card details will be encrypted, so no one else can make use of the details/understand them
2 (a) making a second copy of data, in case original is lost/damaged
(b) files stored remotely
(c) any local problem, will not affect the data as it is stored somewhere else
3 a computer program, designed to reproduce itself, may damage data, or executable files (any three points)

SYSTEMS DEVELOPMENT 1

Section A
1 a 3 a 5 b
2 c 4 d

Section B
1 data requirements, data sources, data collection methods, input methods, validation requirements, data processing requirements (or example), data throughputs, flow charts, outputs, backup strategies (any four points)
2 to help make a decision about whether to go ahead with a project
3

Task	Stage
Issue questionnaires	b
Decide that a data file of customers is needed	a
Present the overall cost of the system	c
Draw system flow charts	d
Describe training needs	c
Specify data requirements.	d

Section C
1 (a) example problems: wrong deliveries, deliveries missed out, difficulty answering enquiries, stock control problems, mistakes in paying employees, files getting lost (any three reasonable points)
(b) interview – allows individuals to express unexpected views, questionnaire: structured answers are obtained, many people can be questioned, observation – first-hand experience of the problems, examine documents – permanent records visible, improvements can be suggested, group discussions – interaction possible, volumetrics – measurable data can be obtained and acted upon (three methods and three reasons)
(c) cost too high, training needs unrealistic, redundancies would be caused, not achievable in the time-scale required, hardware implications (any three points)

SYSTEMS DEVELOPMENT 2

Section A
1 c 3 d 5 d
2 b 4 a

Section B
1 design of: data tables, searches, sorts, interfaces, reports, validation checks, program modules, links/connections (any four points)
2

Task	Stage
Staff training	implementation
Conversion of old data	implementation
Use of invalid data	testing
Determination of data tables	design
Writing program code	implementation

3 (a) pilot running: part of system introduced to see if it performs correctly, parallel running: old and new systems run side by side
(b) advantage: no duplication of effort/get benefits immediately
disadvantage: if there is a problem – no backup system

Section C
1 (a) splitting a problem, into sub-problems
(b) problem easier to solve, easier to test, division of labour, modules can be re-used (any two points)
(c)

central heating system

(d) set temperature – does system bring room to correct temperature?
set timer – does system switch on/off at correct time?
temperature drops – does boiler/pump switch on?
(any three reasonable tests that relate to this system)

SYSTEMS DEVELOPMENT 3

Section A
1 d 3 c 5 b
2 a 4 a

Section B
1 maintenance, bugs/faults, interface, [hardware/platform /operating system (any two of these)]
2 (a) new software usually has added features, these require more computer resources, old hardware may not be adequate
(b) cost of the software, old skills may not be adequate/learning new features, old files may be incompatible
3 keep modules small, keep modules simple, write clear code (or any comment that suggests this), construct modules in a clear/ordered way
4 programs are often very complex, difficult to check all possible circumstances, not cost-effective (any two points)

Section C
1 (a) extra features, changed interface, bugs fixed, improved help, improved documentation, improved performance
(b) tax changes, could require them to do their work in a different way
(c) pay web developer to set up site, pay programmers to get software to accept on-line data, pay service provider, hire more people to deal with extra business
2 (a) consult the client, compare the resulting software against original specification, check for bugs, check the performance/speed, any future improvements
(b) (i) the developer is too close to the project and may miss things, the developer does not see software in realistic action
(ii) the client, because he/she is the one paying for the product, most likely to see what is needed in a realistic setting (any two points)
(iii) questionnaire, interview, discussion/meeting (any two points)

DOCUMENTATION

Section A
1 c 3 b 5 d
2 d 4 c

Section B
1 what the software does, installation instructions, system requirements, how to enter data, form of output data, error messages, tutorial, backing up instructions (any three points)
2 advantages: hypertext – can follow links, up to date, software supplier can gather data about questions, can produce FAQs, can gather commercial information
disadvantages: may need to register, need to be at computer to find out
3 maintenance/updates/ alterations, algorithms, modules/subroutines/functions/ components, link, formulae/functions/macros (two out of three)

Section C
1 (a) examples: specification of the hardware, make of the hardware, applications installed, operating system installed, cable details, protocols, bandwidths
(b) wiring layout/ports on hubs/other hardware
(c) (i) documentation made available on the computer system, accessible by requesting help/selecting help from menu or pressing F1
(ii) saves storage space, easy to find topic required, easy to update (any two points)
(iii) help that is displayed over a particular item, when the mouse cursor hovers over an item
(iv) don't need to be at the computer, laid out in structured way, comprehensive

ALGORITHMS AND FLOW CHARTS

Section A
1 c 3 a 5 a
2 d 4 b

Section B
1 (a) process
(b) tape file
(c) manual input
(d) disk file
(e) paper output
2 an algorithm, program flow chart, pseudocode

Section C
1 (a) • set counter to 0
• car detected
• add 1 to counter
• does counter=maximum?
• close barrier
(b) • car detected leaving
• take 1 from the counter
• between stages 1 and 2 or between stages 3 and 4
2 • input temperature (input box)
• detect temperature (input box)
• check temperature against input value (process box)
• is temperature too low? (decision box)
• 'Yes' and 'No' exits from decision box

- 'Yes' leads to 'turn heater on'
- 'No' loops back to 'detect temperature'
(any five of these points)

COMPUTERS AND WORK

Section A
1 b 3 d 5 b
2 a 4 a

Section B
1 don't get tired, don't go on strike, don't need holidays, don't take breaks, repeat actions exactly, more reliable quality
2 There are lots of suitable examples – make sure that they are properly work-related, such as:
   (a) preparing lessons, keeping pupil records, making presentations, computer assisted learning
   (b) preparing newsletters/posters, keeping accounts, writing sermons
   (c) CAD, (any) calculations
   (d) diagnosis, patient records, drug details
3 (a) better motivation, operate systems more effectively, less likely to lose staff
   (b) training is expensive, need to retrain often, as systems change so quickly (any two points)

Section C
1 (a) less travel, hence money saved, work at time to suit herself, greater freedom where to live
   (b) saves office space, better motivation, 'hot-desking' allows different people to make use of same resources
   (c) distractions from family, need to set up a work room, temptation not to work, less social contact (any two points)
   (d) interact with colleagues to exchange ideas, formal meetings, training (any two points)
2 a modem/router, to connect PC to WAN/Internet

EFFECTS OF INFORMATION TECHNOLOGY

Section A
1 d 3 d 5 b
2 d 4 b

Section B
1 (a) trend towards paying for goods and services by electronic means, such as credit/debit cards, credit transfers (any two points)
   (b) people's habits and preferences may resist change, some people cannot get credit/might not have bank accounts, small transactions – not worth having credit card facilities
2 Electronic Point of Sale – goods are scanned and bills produced at checkout, Electronic Funds Transfer at Point of Sale – allows cashless payment at checkout
3 (a) security issues, records of payments

(b) safer than handling cash, automated so cheaper, less likely to make mistakes, automatically generate accounts
4 obviously there are many possible answers to this, but any three reasonable points such as ATMs, statement generation, accounts, checking transactions/credit limits, advertising, on-line banking, website

Section C
1 (a) itemised bills, no need to carry cash, quicker service, better stock control so more likely to have wanted item in stock (any two points)
   (b) fewer errors, more customers served, easier to set staffing levels, can be linked to stock control
   (c) cashback service
   (d) card scanner/swipe device, bar-code scanner, printer, network interface card (any two points)
2 (a) (i) credit cards: borrow money to pay
       (ii) debit cards: use money that is already in account
       (iii) loyalty cards: collect points when shopping
   (b) data collection, encourages shopper to spend more

HEALTH AND SAFETY

Section A
1 c
2 a
3 a
4 b
5 d

Section B
1

Problem	Solution
Electric shock	regular safety checks on equipment/ ensure no exposed wiring
Backache	ergonomically designed chair/take regular breaks
Monitor radiation	low radiation monitors
Wrist ache	wrist rest, ergonomic keyboard
Neck ache	good posture

2 (a) joint/muscle pain, due to an action being repeated many times
   (b) typing for a long time, together with bad posture
3 uncertainty about ability to cope, frequent changes in work practices, fear of redundancy, excessive expectations of output, excessive monitoring (any three points)

Section C
1 (a) ATC may instruct other plane to go higher as well
   (b) (i) prevents human error, all necessary information

made available to on-board computers, computers react faster than humans (any two points)
       (ii) data may be insufficient/inaccurate, hardware failure could lead to wrong decisions, software may have faults in it, over-reliance on system by pilot (any two points)
       (iii) real-time allows immediate response, to input data, delays could be disastrous
2 site monitors away from windows, anti-glare screens, larger screens, arrange regular eye tests, better monitors/high refresh rates, adjust lighting levels (any three points)

COMPUTER MISUSE

Section A
1 a 3 b 5 a
2 c 4 c

Section B
1 data, shopping habits, type of house, salary/work performance/opinions of bosses/tax paid, (any two points), the Inland Revenue, tax
2 data stored in large quantities, can be combined, can be searched in various ways
3 there are many possibilities, any three reasonable items such as: any personal details such as name/address etc (only one of these), work record, exam results, class/group, date of entry, roll number

Section C
1 invasion of privacy, details may be passed to someone else, criminals may find out personal information, the state may find out information (any two points)
2 (a) permission to use software, not ownership
   (b) permission to use software throughout an organisation/site – no restriction on number of machines using it
   (c) deprives software companies of income, therefore they cannot afford to develop new software
3 (a) statement/document where employee agrees to the conditions for computer use
   (b) there are many possible correct responses, some examples are: playing games, copying software, sending private e-mails, running own business using firm's resources, installing software, visiting undesirable websites (any four reasonable points)

DATA PROTECTION ACT

Section A
1 d 3 a 5 b
2 b 4 a

Section B
1 Police records, security service records, medical records.

2 individual, about whom data is stored, which is personal, able to be identified from the data (any three points)
3 a person or organisation that holds personal data, on a computer system
4 Data Protection Registrar, government
5 data obtained legally, can view data stored about them, data not passed to others, data not kept longer than necessary, data kept securely (any three points)

Section C
1 (a) data has been passed to other companies, without permission
   (b) Stephanie has not ticked box, disallowing the passing on of data
   (c) DPA requires data to be made available to data subject, so give Stephanie a print-out of data held
2 exemptions to the Act, include Inland Revenue
3 (a) data is used for statistical purposes, individuals not identifiable
   (b) may need personal details of patient, if patient is in danger/facts needed to be able to provide the most appropriate treatment

USING THE INTERNET

Section A
1 d 3 c 5 c
2 b 4 a

Section B
1 (a) ISP/internet service provider
   (b) examples such as: news, stock market reports, weather, discussion groups, search engine links, job finder, webpage builders (any four reasonable points)
2 (a) speed at which data is transmitted
   (b) (i) ISDN/leased line
       (ii) router
3 locally installed e-mail software – access to ISP account/many features/may run faster than web-based software, web-based e-mail software – available from any connected computer

Section C
1 (a)

Feature	Letter
Command button	D
Text box	C
Hyperlink	B
URL	A

   (b) browser
2 (a) HTML/hypertext mark-up language
   (b) HTML editor
   (c) modem, computer uses digital signals, telephone system uses analogue signals, modem converts A→D and D→A

FEATURES OF THE INTERNET

Section A
1 c 3 a 5 a
2 d 4 d

Section B
1 (a) hypertext mark-up language, language for defining a web page, controls appearance of web page, instructions to browser (any two points)
  (b) tags
  (c) control how the text is displayed, in the user's browser
2 item on a web page, that can be clicked on, to send browser to/provides link to another page/part of page (any two points)
3 database software, store of website details, provided on a website, allows enquiries to be made (any two points)

Section C
1 (a) not restricted to opening hours, can access account from anywhere, cheaper service because of fewer overheads incurred by bank, can set up direct debits/standing orders /payments on-line, no standing in queues (any three points)
  (b) save money, by cutting staff, bigger customer base, as world-wide access, as customers get faster service (any two points)
  (c) (i) unauthorised access, to computer files
      (ii) firewalls, encryption, passwords, keep sensitive information off-line, change passwords frequently (any three points)
2 low overheads/need few people to run the operation, can update site quickly, can offer surplus holidays straight away (any two points)

THE INTERNET

Section A
1 b 3 a 5 b
2 c 4 d

Section B
1 network, of computers/networks, world-wide, WAN, can communicate (any three points)
2 (a) conducting business, using computer communication /the Internet
  (b) attractively designed site, site easy to navigate, ability to fulfil orders, speed of fulfilling orders, after sales service (any three points)
3 (a) rules, for communication, between devices (any two points)
  (b) FTP/file transfer protocol
4 computer: digital/on or off; telephone: analogue/varying voltage

Section C
1 (a) A: e-mail address of recipient
      B: e-mail address of someone to whom a copy is being sent
      C: subject to summarise what the e-mail is about
      D: message body – the message itself
  (b) to attach computer files to the message.
2 (a) load e-mail software, enter user ID, enter password, select new message/compose, enter recipient's e-mail address, enter subject, write message, click send, log off
  (b) mail may contain a virus, may encourage spam (any one point)

DRAWBACKS OF THE INTERNET

Section A
1 a 3 b 5 b
2 c 4 d

Section B
1 block, filter, URL/address/IP address, copyright.

2 (a)

Search string	Number of hits reported
London buses	298,000
"London buses"	12,300
London	33,100,000

  (b) the more specific the search string, the fewer hits (or reverse argument), more words bring fewer matches, use of quotation marks requires exact match

Section C
1 (a) activities: accessing undesirable sites, excessive personal e-mail, maintaining own website in company time reasons: wasting time, bring company into disrepute, offend others, clog up bandwidth, clog up e-mail servers (any six points)
  (b) e-mail is not secure, it passes through many servers, it can be accessed at many places (any two points)
  (c) credit/debit card details may be accessed, by hackers, account may be used fraudulently, not confident that goods will be delivered, or of good quality (any four points)

BENEFITS OF THE INTERNET

Section A
1 b 3 b 5 a
2 b 4 d

Section B
1 text, graphics, movies, sounds (any three points from this list), applets
2 (a) no need to leave home, wide range of goods, can shop internationally, can save money, rapid delivery may be possible (any three points)
  (b) security issues, vendor may not be reliable, may be difficult to get in touch with vendor if problems, may have to wait for delivery if sent from abroad (any three points)
3 inadequate infrastructure (networks/ISPs) where they live, do not possess computer equipment, unable to use the technology

Section C
1 (a) accessible, can search world-wide, latest research available, material might not be published elsewhere, easy to paste in reference material (any three points)
  (b) search engine
  (c) might be out of date, not on the exact topic required, might be unreliable (any two points)
  (d) check with different sources, check date when site last updated, consider whether site is likely to be authoritative – a university site rather than an individual (any two reasoned points)
2 (a) advertising, collecting customer data, communicating, conduct business transactions, on-line display of goods/services, exploring new markets, provide customer support (any three points)
  (b) (i) intranet
      (ii) on-line training, public information /newsletters, to look up details that might help in the work, such as items in stock (or suitable alternative), links to outside sites of interest, other suitable answers (any two points)
      (iii) seperate server may be required, staff to keep system up to date, or outsource the job, expertise required (any two points)

LETTS EDUCATIONAL
The Chiswick Centre
414 Chiswick High Road
London W4 5TF
Tel: 020 8996 3333
Fax: 020 8742 8390
Email: mail@lettsed.co.uk
Website: www.letts-education.com

C | These are GCSE style questions. Answer all parts of the questions.

1 Cyril's Travel is a bus company. It employs 30 drivers and has 20 buses. The bus drivers have to have a public service vehicle licence and be between 21 and 65 years of age. They are paid an hourly wage according to how much driving experience they have.

(a) On a separate piece of paper, design an application form that a driver would have to fill in when applying for a job with Cyril's Travel. (6 marks)

(b) All the data from the application form has to be entered into a database. The company wants to make sure that the data is accurate. They do not want people's names spelt wrongly. Describe how the data entry clerks can make sure that the data is accurate and without spelling mistakes.

....

....

.... (4 marks)

(c) The date of birth entered can partly be checked by the computer. Describe **two** checks that the computer could carried out.

....

....

.... (4 marks)

(d) Cyril's Travel keeps details of when the vehicles are serviced in its database. The buses are serviced every six months or when they have travelled 15,000 miles. The operator enters the reference numbers of those buses that need servicing this week. Describe the checks that the software will need to carry out to ensure that the buses selected are the correct ones.

....

....

.... (4 marks)

Score   /18

How well did you do?
0–11	Try again
12–17	Getting there
18–29	Good work
30–34	Excellent!

TOTAL SCORE   /34

**For more on this topic
see pages 46–49 of your Success Guide**

FILES

A

Choose just one answer, a, b, c or d.

1 Some database systems find records on a disk by calculating the disk address from the key field. Such files are said to be
(a) serial access   (c) random access
(b) indexed sequential   (d) sequential.
(1 mark)

2 A record number is entered into a database enquiry screen. The software is able to retrieve the correct record straight away without having to check all the previous records. This type of access is called
(a) serial access   (c) sequential access
(b) direct access   (d) indexed sequential access. (1 mark)

3 One advantage of random access files is
(a) the data are in order
(b) the data are always up to date

(c) the data are more secure
(d) the data can be retrieved directly, without having to examine all other records. (1 mark)

4 Serial files
(a) store data in key field order
(b) find data by means of an index
(c) automatically store new records in the correct location
(d) store data in no particular order. (1 mark)

5 A flight booking system requires database records to be found quickly so that they can be updated straight away. The best form of file access for this is
(a) serial access   (c) sequential access
(b) random access   (d) indexed sequential access. (1 mark)

Score   /5

B

Answer all parts of all questions.

1 Here are some situations where computer files are produced or used. For each one, state whether it is a serial, sequential or random access file. In each case, make a brief comment to explain why it is that type of file.

	Situation	Serial, sequential or random access	Reason
a	a clothes shop records each sale as it is made		
b	a hotel stores details of its rooms to allow on–line bookings to be made		
c	a builder's merchant stores details of all its products		
d	a data–logging system stores details of air temperatures over a period of a month		
e	a sorted file of library loans is used to update the stock file		

(10 marks)

2 From the situations described in the last question, identify two transaction files and one master file.

Transaction file 1: ....   Transaction file 2: ....

Master file: ....

(3 marks)

Score /13

50

C **These are GCSE style questions. Answer all parts of the questions.**

1 Ian needs to increase the credit limit on his credit card. He telephones the credit card company. A recorded message asks him to key in his 16-digit credit card number using the telephone keypad. He is then held in a queuing system until a representative can speak to him. The representative has all his details ready as they are read from a random access computer file.

(a) Give **two** reasons why Ian's details are stored in a random access file.

....

....

.... (4 marks)

(b) State what type of backing storage device the credit card company must use to store Ian's details and why this type of device is necessary.

....

.... (2 marks)

(c) Explain how the 16-digit card number is used to access Ian's details.

....

....

.... (3 marks)

(d) Briefly explain how a record is located in a random access file.

....

.... (2 marks)

2 **(a)** A serial file has 1,000 records. Explain how a computer can find the 20th record.

....

....

.... (3 marks)

(b) The serial file is sorted into key field order. Explain how the computer system would find a particular record.

....

....

.... (3 marks)

Score /17

How well did you do?

0–12 Try again
13–18 Getting there
19–29 Good work
30–35 Excellent!

TOTAL SCORE /35

**For more on this topic
see pages 50–51 of your Success Guide**

FILE PROCESSING

A

Choose just one answer, a, b, c or d.

1 Before a transaction file can be used to update a master file, it must be
(a) searched   (c) validated
(b) sorted   (d) verified.   **(1 mark)**

2 A common method of keeping data safe when updating data file tapes is
(a) incremental backups
(b) archiving
(c) file generations
(d) off-line storage.   **(1 mark)**

3 When a transaction file is used to update a master file, the new master file is called
(a) the father file
(b) the grandfather file
(c) the backup file
(d) the son file.   **(1 mark)**

4 When two files in order are combined to produce another single file also in order, the process is called
(a) updating
(b) backing up
(c) archiving
(d) merging.   **(1 mark)**

5 A transaction tape file is used to update a master file, also on tape. At the end of this update process, how many files will there be?
(a) 2
(b) 1
(c) 4
(d) 3   **(1 mark)**

Score   /5

B

Answer all parts of all questions.

1 When students arrive each day at a college, they register by swiping their identity cards. Each arrival is stored as it happens, in a registration file. A batch process is then used each day to update the student records file.

MOORMINSTER
UNIVERSITY
STUDENT CARD
Bob Smith

The following actions are used in the update process:

compare the key fields, write updated record to new student file, read a record from the registration file, sort registration file, read a record from the student file

Rewrite these processes in the correct order.

....

....

.... **(5 marks)**

2 The college receives a batch of applications from prospective students every day. These are entered into the current_applications file by the office staff. Each day, the staff have to merge the new current_applications data into the master_applications file. Explain how the merge operation will be carried out.

....

....

.... **(8 marks)**

Score   /13

C These are GCSE style questions. Answer all parts of the questions.

1 (a) The system flow chart below shows a typical file updating process. Label each of the symbols with the appropriate words, taken from this list: **update, new transaction file, master file, updated master file, sorted transaction file, sort.** (6 marks)

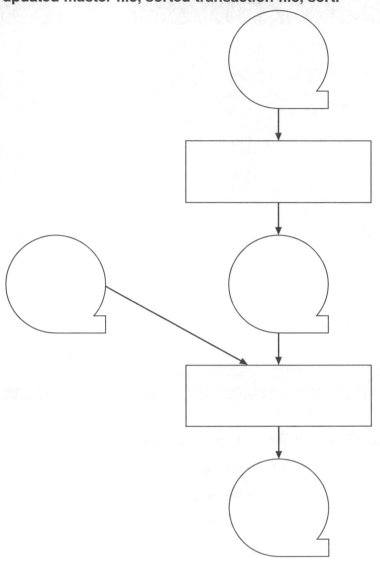

(b) At the end of this process, one of the files could be referred to as the 'father' file and another the 'son' file. Label these on the diagram. (2 marks)

(c) Grandfather, father and son files are part of a file generation system. Explain why many organisations use this system.

....

.... (4 marks)

Score /12

How well did you do?

0–10	Try again
11–15	Getting there
16–25	Good work
26–30	Excellent!

TOTAL SCORE /30

For more on this topic see pages 52–53 of your Success Guide

A **Choose just one answer, a, b, c or d.**

1 Screen output is essential when
(a) it is important that the output is up to date
(b) the output is in colour
(c) the output is moving
(d) the output needs to be kept for the future.
(1 mark)

2 Hard copy is needed when the output
(a) needs to be in black and white
(b) needs to be kept for the future
(c) needs to be taken away
(d) is larger than will fit onto one screen.
(1 mark)

3 When computer output is in the form of text, it can be usefully summarised by using
(a) bullet points
(b) charts
(c) text fields
(d) white space.
(1 mark)

4 This question has been written in a certain type of font. It can be described as
(a) bold
(b) sans-serif
(c) serif
(d) italic.
(1 mark)

5 A survey has been carried out to find the percentage of people who intend to vote for each party in an election. The proportions can best be shown as
(a) a bar chart
(b) a line graph
(c) a pie chart
(d) a scatter chart.
(1 mark)

Score /5

B **Answer all parts of all questions.**

1 Which four of the following can be forms of computer output?

(a) a mouse click ☐

(b) a swipe card ☐

(c) a red traffic signal ☐

(d) an ATM key pad ☐

(e) a pay slip ☐

(f) a list of occupied rooms in a hotel ☐

(g) a motor race lap time ☐

(4 marks)

2 Describe three ways in which a database report can help to present data so that it is organised and easy to follow.

....

....

.... (3 marks)

3 (a) Explain what is meant by hard copy.

.... (2 marks)

(b) Give two reasons why hard copy might be required from a computer system.

....

.... (2 marks)

(c) Give two reasons why hard copy from a computer may be an unsuitable means of presenting results.

.... (2 marks)

Score /13

C **These are GCSE style questions. Answer all parts of the questions.**

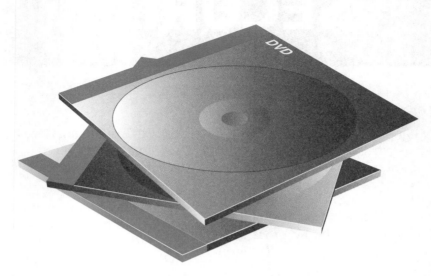

1 David's DVDs is a new e-business that sells DVDs to customers over the Internet. Part of their website allows customers to search for a particular DVD title or category and display a list of those available that match the customer's requirements.

(a) On a separate piece of paper, draw a simple diagram of a suitable web page that shows clearly the enquiry and the results. It must also be able to link to further details and, if necessary, add the DVD to an order. (6 marks)

(b) Label your diagram to show

(i) an input area

(ii) an output area

(iii) a part of the screen that will not change, whatever the enquiry. (3 marks)

(c) State, with reasons, **two** other forms of output that would be useful to add to the website in addition to enquiry and ordering information.

....

....

.... (3 marks)

2 (a) Explain the difference between a serif and a sans-serif font.

.... (1 mark)

(b) Explain why many presentations display numerical information in the form of charts or graphs.

.... (2 marks)

Score   /15

How well did you do?

0–10   Try again
11–16 Getting there
17–26 Good work
27–33 Excellent!

TOTAL SCORE   **/33**

**For more on this topic
see pages 54–55 of your Success Guide**

55

SECURITY

A

Choose just one answer, a, b, c or d.

1 Which of the following is a sensible precaution against viruses?
- (a) don't use downloaded executable files
- (b) don't let employees make their own applications
- (c) don't download wallpaper from the Internet
- (d) always disallow macros in word processed documents
(1 mark)

2 A computer virus
- (a) always damages data
- (b) is likely to damage hardware
- (c) is designed to copy itself
- (d) only infects data files.
(1 mark)

3 The most reliable way of ensuring that data is not lost because of malicious activities is to
- (a) install anti-virus software

- (b) carry out regular backups
- (c) not open e-mails
- (d) install a firewall.
(1 mark)

4 Hacking is
- (a) an attempt to infect files with a virus
- (b) an attempt to access files without authorisation
- (c) an attempt to damage data
- (d) an attempt to alter data.
(1 mark)

5 Which of these methods is most likely to reduce the chances of a virus problem in a network?
- (a) backing up data regularly
- (b) preventing the access of e-mails
- (c) installing anti-virus software
- (d) installation of a firewall
(1 mark)

Score   /5

B

Answer all parts of all questions.

1 List three ways in which data could be lost accidentally.

....

.... (3 marks)

2 Fill in the gaps.

In order to prevent unauthorised alteration to data, screensavers can be protected with a

.... to prevent their being switched off. Files can be made ....–only.

When transmitting data across a network, the data can be .... to prevent unauthorised

users understanding it. .... can be installed to prevent outsiders from gaining access to

a network. In case there is a problem, a .... can be maintained to produce evidence of

who has accessed sensitive files.
(5 marks)

3 State three ways in which important data can be physically protected.

....

.... (3 marks)

4 A company makes regular backups of its data. Explain how it can best make sure that the backups are safe.

.... (2 marks)

Score   /13

56

C These are GCSE style questions. Answer all parts of the questions.

1 David's DVDs sells DVDs on-line via the Internet. When customers buy DVDs, they enter their credit card details. Some customers are worried that hackers might gain access to their credit card details and make fraudulent transactions on their account.

(a) Explain what is meant by hacking.

....

.... (2 marks)

(b) Explain what David's DVDs can do to reassure customers that their details are safe.

....

.... (2 marks)

2 (a) Explain what is meant by **backing up** data.

....

.... (2 marks)

(b) Someone suggests that an on-line backup would be convenient. Explain what is meant by an on-line backup.

.... (1 mark)

(c) Explain why an on-line backup provides extra security.

....

.... (2 marks)

3 Explain what is meant by a computer virus and why viruses are a danger to computer data.

....

.... (3 marks)

Score   /12

How well did you do?

0–10   Try again
11–15 Getting there
16–25 Good work
26–30 Excellent!

TOTAL SCORE   /30

For more on this topic
see pages 56–57 of your Success Guide

SYSTEMS DEVELOPMENT 1

A Choose just one answer, a, b, c or d.

1 Which of the following is a job normally carried out by a systems analyst?
(a) producing a program specification
(b) writing the program code
(c) testing the program
(d) leading the programming project (1 mark)

2 Deciding where the data will come from in a project is looked at during the
(a) design
(b) implementation
(c) analysis
(d) problem identification. (1 mark)

3 System flow charts will usually be drawn during the
(a) analysis
(b) design

(c) evaluation
(d) implementation. (1 mark)

4 When planning a project, staffing issues will be principally addressed in the
(a) design
(b) analysis
(c) maintenance phase
(d) feasibility study. (1 mark)

5 Which of these is likely to take place during the investigation stage of systems development?
(a) design of data input screens
(b) examination of paperwork
(c) writing of code
(d) training of staff (1 mark)

Score   /5

B Answer all parts of all questions.

1 Part of the systems life cycle involves the analysis stage. State four issues that need to be looked at during this stage.

....

.... (4 marks)

2 Explain the purpose of a feasibility study.

.... (1 mark)

3 Some of the early stages in systems development are:

(a) problem definition   (c) feasibility study

(b) investigation   (d) analysis

Enter the correct letter in the table to indicate where each task takes place.

Task	Stage
Issue questionnaires	
Decide that a data file of customers is needed	
Present the overall cost of the system	
Draw system flow charts	
Describe training needs	
Specify data requirements	

(6 marks)
Score   /11

These are GCSE style questions. Answer all parts of the questions.

1 (a) A newsagent is considering installing a computer system. Describe **three** problems that the newsagent may have that could be solved by using a computer system.

....

....

.... (3 marks)

(b) A systems analyst is appointed to investigate the newsagent's business. Describe **three** ways that a systems analyst could find out the necessary facts in order to plan a computer system. For each way, describe the benefits of that method.

....

....

....

....

....

.... (6 marks)

(c) The systems analyst produces a **feasibility study**. The newsagent may then decide not to go ahead with the proposed system. Give **three** reasons why a computer system may be rejected at this stage.

....

....

.... (3 marks)

Score   /12

How well did you do?

0–9	Try again
10–14	Getting there
15–23	Good work
24–28	Excellent!

TOTAL SCORE   /28

For more on this topic see pages 60–61 of your Success Guide

SYSTEMS DEVELOPMENT 2

A **Choose just one answer, a, b, c or d.**

1 **Which of the following is likely to take place in the design stage of systems development?**
(a) testing the software
(b) filling in questionnaires
(c) determining the content of data tables
(d) parallel running (1 mark)

2 **Implementation is likely to include**
(a) deciding the format of reports
(b) converting existing data
(c) deciding on validation techniques
(d) estimating the volume of work. (1 mark)

3 **When a program is tested by a group of trusted users, this is called**
(a) alpha testing
(b) system testing

(c) module testing
(d) beta testing. (1 mark)

4 **The evaluation of a computer system should always involve**
(a) the user
(b) the programmer
(c) the analyst
(d) the technical author. (1 mark)

5 **When a new system is run side-by-side with the old system, this is called**
(a) pilot running
(b) all at once
(c) module testing
(d) parallel running. (1 mark)

Score /5

B **Answer all parts of all questions.**

1 State four tasks that will be performed in the design stage of systems development.

....

.... (4 marks)

2 For each of the following tasks, state the stage of systems development where it occurs.

Task	Stage
Staff training	
Conversion of old data	
Use of invalid data	
Determination of data tables	
Writing program code	

(5 marks)

3 (a) When a new system is finished, it can be introduced by pilot running or parallel running. Explain how these approaches differ from each other.

.... (2 marks)

(b) Another method of introducing a new system is 'once and for all'. Describe one advantage and one disadvantage of this method.

.... (2 marks)

Score /13

C

These are GCSE style questions. Answer all parts of the questions.

1 A team of programmers is working on a system that provides computer control of a central heating system. They are using top-down design methods.

(a) Explain what is meant by top-down design.

....

.... (2 marks)

(b) Describe **two** benefits of using top-down design methods.

....

.... (2 marks)

(c) The following diagram shows some of the modules that make up the central heating control system.

central heating system

central heating control

check temperature

set timings

Add these other modules in the correct places:

• switch boiler on or off

• switch pump on or off

• operate heating system

• set temperature

• user input. (5 marks)

(d) Describe three tests that could be carried out to check that the control system works correctly.

....

....

.... (3 marks)

Score   /12

How well did you do?

0–10   Try again
11–15   Getting there
16–25   Good work
26–30   Excellent!

TOTAL SCORE   /30

**For more on this topic
see pages 62–63 of your Success Guide**

SYSTEMS DEVELOPMENT 3

A

Choose just one answer, a, b, c or d.

1 What circumstance would require a software developer to alter a program without any extra charge?
(a) New laws require a new feature in the software.
(b) The client wants a different interface.
(c) The client changes the computer hardware.
(d) A bug needs to be fixed. (1 mark)

2 When a program is complete, it often has to be worked on again at a later stage. This is called
(a) maintenance (c) implementation
(b) evaluation (d) analysis (1 mark)

3 Why is it a good idea if programs are built up from small modules?
(a) the finished program is smaller
(b) the finished program runs faster

(c) maintenance is easier
(d) there is less testing to do (1 mark)

4 Which of these circumstances is likely to require program maintenance
(a) the organisation changes to a new operating system
(b) the program is being abandoned
(c) a new system is introduced
(d) new users are appointed (1 mark)

5 Why do some people find software upgrades a nuisance?
(a) often they are not tested fully
(b) often they require new hardware
(c) often they have lengthy installation procedures
(d) they don't need the new features. (1 mark)

Score /5

B

Answer all parts of all questions.

1 Fill in the gaps.

Altering software after it has been implemented is known as program .... This work may be needed if there are still some .... in the software. The client might need some changes to the .... because the staff are finding the software hard to use. The client may also decide to change the computer .... or .... and that will require the software to be changed. (5 marks)

2 (a) Explain why a new version of a software product often requires users to change their hardware.

....

.... (3 marks)

(b) State three other reasons why new versions of software can be a nuisance to users.

....

.... (3 marks)

3 State three ways that programmers can make sure that maintenance is made as easy as possible.

....

.... (3 marks)

4 Explain why most programs are released with some bugs, even after extensive testing.

.... (2 marks)

Score /16

62

C **These are GCSE style questions. Answer all parts of the questions.**

1 A firm of accountants uses specially written software to calculate the tax liabilities of its clients. When it is delivered, it works well and helps them run their business more effectively. After a year, they ask the software developers to make some changes.

(a) Give **three** reasons why the accountants may require the changes.

....

.... (3 marks)

(b) Describe why government action might require changes to be made to their software.

....

.... (2 marks)

(c) The accountants decide to offer some of their services on-line to clients, so that they can send their information via the Internet. Describe why this would cost the accountants extra money.

....

....

.... (3 marks)

2 (a) A software developer is evaluating a computer system that he has produced. Describe **three** important considerations that he will have to remember.

....

....

.... (3 marks)

(b) The evaluation should not be carried out by the developer alone.

(i) Explain why this is the case.

....

.... (2 marks)

(ii) State who else should be involved in the evaluation and explain the reasons for this.

....

.... (2 marks)

(iii) Describe two ways in which the other person can provide information for the evaluation.

....

.... (2 marks)

Score   /17

How well did you do?

0–13	Try again
14–19	Getting there
20–32	Good work
33–38	Excellent!

TOTAL SCORE   /38

For more on this topic see pages 64–65 of your Success Guide

DOCUMENTATION

A Choose just one answer, a, b, c or d.

1 Which of these is likely to be in the user documentation?
(a) test data
(c) backing up procedures
(b) program code
(d) file structures (1 mark)

2 Which of these is likely to be in the technical documentation?
(a) backing up procedures
(b) tutorial
(c) glossary
(d) test data (1 mark)

3 A program algorithm is likely to be found in
(a) the user guide
(b) the technical documentation
(c) the data structures
(d) the feasibility study. (1 mark)

4 On-line documentation has many advantages over paper documentation. Which of these is not such an advantage?
(a) hypertext links can be used
(b) it is easy to update
(c) it can be read anywhere
(d) it is easy to search (1 mark)

5 On-line documentation often has technical words highlighted in a different colour. Clicking on the word leads to further explanation. This is called
(a) tool tips
(b) a tutorial
(c) context-sensitive help
(d) hypertext. (1 mark)

Score   /5

B Answer all parts of all questions.

1 State three items that would be in the user documentation for a piece of software.

....

....

.... (3 marks)

2 Give two advantages and two disadvantages of web-based documentation over paper manuals.

Advatage 1: ....

Advantage 2: ....

Disadvantage 1: ....

Disadvantage 2: .... (4 marks)

SUPER OFFICE USER GUIDE

3 Fill in the blanks.

Programs need to be documented to help with later .... The technical documentation

contains .... which are the steps taken by the program to solve the problem. The

program will probably be written in many small .... and it is important to document how

these .... together. If the software is based on a customised spreadsheet, it is necessary

to describe all the .... and .... used to perform calculations.   (6 marks)

Score   /13

C These are GCSE style questions. Answer all parts of the questions.

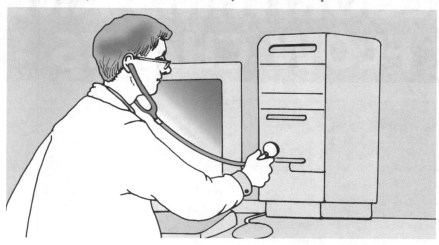

1 A doctor's surgery has had a computer network installed. The network manager has been given documentation about the new network set-up.

(a) What are **four** items of information that would be in the network manager's documentation?

....

.... (4 marks)

(b) State one item of information that would require a diagram to be provided.

.... (1 mark)

(c) The users are given different documentation with some of it available on-line.

  (i) Explain what is meant by on-line documentation.

  ....

  .... (2 marks)

  (ii) Describe **two** advantages of on-line documentation over paper documentation.

  ....

  .... (2 marks)

  (iii) Part of the help provided to users is in the form of **tool tips**. Explain what tool tips are.

  ....

  .... (2 marks)

  (iv) The documentation is also provided in a printed manual. Give **one** advantage of providing documentation this way.

  .... (1 mark)

Score   /12

How well did you do?
0–10   Try again
11–15 Getting there
16–25 Good work
26–30 Excellent!

TOTAL SCORE   /30

**For more on this topic
see pages 66–67 of your Success Guide**

ALGORITHMS AND FLOW CHARTS

A Choose just one answer, a, b, c or d.

1 The steps necessary to solve a problem and used to design a computer program are called
(a) a system (c) an algorithm
(b) data flow (d) a process. (1 mark)

2 An algorithm can be described by using a series of program-like statements, but without writing the program. This is called
(a) high level code
(b) low level code
(c) object code
(d) pseudocode. (1 mark)

3 A diagram that represents an algorithm is called
(a) a program flow chart
(b) a systems flow chart

(c) a data flow diagram
(d) an entity relation diagram (1 mark)

4 A decision box in a program flow chart has
(a) one input and one output
(b) one input and two outputs
(c) two inputs and one output
(d) two inputs and two outputs. (1 mark)

5 In a systems flow chart, a process is represented by
(a) a rectangle
(b) a diamond
(c) a cylinder
(d) a parallelogram. (1 mark)

Score /5

B Answer all parts of all questions.

1 Here are five symbols that may be used in a systems flow chart. They represent: manual input, a process, a disk file, paper output, a tape file, but not in that order. Give the symbols their correct descriptions.

Symbol   Description   Symbol   Description

(a) .... (c) ....

(b) .... (d) ....

(e) ....

(5 marks)

2 Fill in the blanks.

The steps taken by a program to carry out some process are called .... This can be

expressed as a diagram which is called a ....

Alternatively, the steps can be set out as a series of statements that look rather like program code.

This is called .... (4 marks)

Score /9

66

C These are GCSE style questions. Answer all parts of the questions.

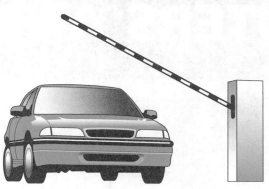

1 (a) A car park has a sensor that detects each car as it enters through the barrier. A computer controls the barrier. The computer software uses an algorithm to operate this function. The algorithm contains the following statements:

- does counter=maximum?

- set counter to 0

- car detected

- close barrier

- add 1 to counter

Add the correct statements to the flow chart boxes on the right. (5 marks)

(b) This algorithm does not take into account cars leaving the car park. What **two** statements would need to be added to the algorithm and at what point?

……..…………………………..………

……..…………………………..………

……..…………………………..……… (3 marks)

2 A computer is used to control the temperature of liquid entering a manufacturing process. A heater is turned on if the liquid is too cold. The operator has first to set the correct temperature. On a separate piece of paper, draw a flow chart to show how the computer would operate this system.

(5 marks)

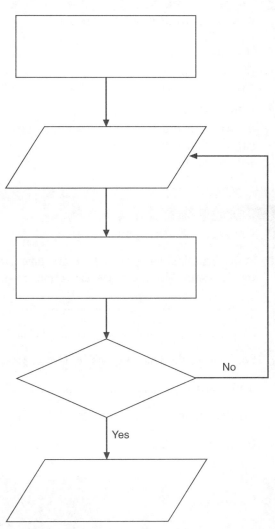

Score /13

How well did you do?

0–8	Try again
9–16	Getting there
17–21	Good work
22–27	Excellent!

TOTAL SCORE /27

For more on this topic see pages 68–69 of your Success Guide

COMPUTERS AND WORK

A

Choose just one answer, a, b, c or d.

1 An ATM is likely to be provided by
  (a) an insurance company
  (b) a bank
  (c) a travel agent
  (d) a doctor's surgery.   (1 mark)

2 The work done by a typesetter is now largely done with what type of software?
  (a) DTP
  (b) word processors
  (c) spreadsheet
  (d) presentation   (1 mark)

3 Who is likely to write the program documentation for a big new project?
  (a) a programmer
  (b) a systems analyst
  (c) a systems administrator
  (d) a technical author   (1 mark)

4 Many factory processes are carried out by robots. An advantage of using robots is that
  (a) they are good at doing repetitive tasks accurately
  (b) they are more adaptable than humans
  (c) they don't break down
  (d) they don't need instructions.   (1 mark)

5 Hospitals use computer techniques to scan patients' bodies. This is called
  (a) CAD   (c) CAM
  (b) CAT   (d) CAL.   (1 mark)

Score   /5

B

Answer all parts of all questions.

1 Many manufacturing processes are now carried out by computer-controlled machines or robots. List four reasons why machines can often do production line jobs better than humans.

....

.... (4 marks)

2 For each of the following people, give one example of how computers can be of help in carrying out their work.

(a) teacher ....

(b) clergyman ....

(c) engineer ....

(d) doctor .... (4 marks)

3 (a) State three benefits of a company providing regular IT training for its workforce.

....

....

.... (3 marks)

(b) Explain why some companies choose not to provide frequent training.

....

.... (2 marks)

Score   /13

C These are GCSE style questions. Answer all parts of the questions.

1 Cassie is an editor. Two days each week she works from home, using her computer, which is connected to the Internet and to her office network.

(a) List **three** advantages **to Cassie** of working at home instead of at the office.

....

....

.... (3 marks)

(b) List **three** advantages **to the publishing company** in letting Cassie work from home.

....

....

.... (3 marks)

(c) List **two** disadvantages of working from home.

....

.... (2 marks)

(d) Explain why Cassie still needs to visit the office personally on other days.

....

.... (2 marks)

2 Apart from a PC with the usual peripherals, explain what extra hardware Cassie would need at home to allow her to carry out her job.

.... (2 marks)

Score   /12

How well did you do?

0–10	Try again
11–15	Getting there
16–25	Good work
26–30	Excellent!

TOTAL SCORE   /30

For more on this topic see pages 72–73 of your Success Guide

EFFECTS OF INFORMATION TECHNOLOGY

A

Choose just one answer, a, b, c or d.

1 In a supermarket, the system that is used to transfer money from a cardholder's account to the supermarket's account is called
(a) EPOS
(c) OCR
(b) OMR
(d) EFTPOS.
(1 mark)

2 A loyalty card can benefit a shop because it
(a) results in faster service
(b) allows the production of itemised bills
(c) speeds up service at the tills
(d) allows the collection of data about shopping habits.
(1 mark)

3 An advantage to a customer of a store using an EFTPOS system is
(a) prices are reduced
(b) bills are more accurate
(c) stock control is carried out more efficiently
(d) customers need not carry as much cash.
(1 mark)

4 Shoppers sometimes like loyalty cards because
(a) they help shorten queues
(b) they can get special offers with them
(c) they reduce prices
(d) they help the supermarket to keep goods fresher.
(1 mark)

5 A cashless society is **unlikely** to happen because
(a) credit card fraud means cash is safer
(b) not everyone has a bank account
(c) the computers of different banks cannot pass data to each other
(d) it is too expensive to install swipe machines in all supermarkets.
(1 mark)

Score /5

B

Answer all parts of all questions.

1 (a) Explain what is meant by a cashless society.

....
(2 marks)

(b) State two reasons why the cashless society might never happen.

....
(2 marks)

2 Explain the difference between EPOS and EFTPOS.

....
....
(2 marks)

3 (a) State two advantages to an employee of having salary payments made straight into the bank.

....
....
(2 marks)

(b) State two advantages to an employer of paying the salary of employees straight into their bank accounts.

....
....
(2 marks)

4 State three ways that a bank might use information technology.

....
....
(3 marks)

Score /13

These are GCSE style questions. Answer all parts of the questions.

1 Bilko's is a large chain of stores that sells a wide variety of household goods. At each of their stores, they allow payment for goods by credit or debit card. Goods are scanned at the checkout before payment. Bilko's is planning to introduce a loyalty card scheme.

(a) State **two** advantages for the customer of having EFTPOS terminals.

....

.... (2 marks)

(b) State **two** advantages to Bilko's of having EFTPOS terminals.

....

.... (2 marks)

(c) Apart from allowing for the payment of goods, state **one** other service that Bilko's can provide customers with its EFTPOS facilities.

.... (1 mark)

(d) State **two** items of hardware required at an EFTPOS terminal apart from the till.

....

.... (2 marks)

2 (a) Explain the purposes of the following.

(i) credit cards ....

(ii) debit cards ....

(iii) loyalty cards .... (3 marks)

(b) Describe **two** reasons why Bilko's might benefit from introducing loyalty cards.

....

.... (2 marks)

Score   /12

How well did you do?

0–10   Try again
11–15 Getting there
16–25 Good work
26–30 Excellent!

TOTAL SCORE   **/30**

For more on this topic see pages 74–75 of your Success Guide

HEALTH AND SAFETY

A Choose just one answer, a, b, c or d.

1 Which of these is least likely to reduce the risk of repetitive strain injury when working at a computer?
(a) a wrist rest
(b) regular breaks
(c) an anti-glare screen
(d) a well-designed keyboard   (1 mark)

2 A good way to avoid back problems when using a computer is to
(a) take regular breaks
(b) use an ergonomically designed keyboard
(c) use a wrist rest
(d) use a suitably sized monitor.   (1 mark)

3 A disadvantage of the increased use of computers at work is
(a) people need retraining at regular intervals
(b) there are usually redundancies
(c) people have less job satisfaction
(d) people have less interesting work to do.
          (1 mark)

4 Which of the following is most likely to be a safety hazard for computer workers?
(a) electric shocks from a keyboard
(b) trailing electrical leads
(c) a badly adjusted monitor
(d) poor choice of background colours in a word processor   (1 mark)

5 Some computer-controlled systems have serious safety implications. What is the best way to guard against a system failure?
(a) thorough alpha testing of the software
(b) making sure that the hardware is up to date
(c) having a backup computer system
(d) providing a human backup system (1 mark)

Score   /5

B Answer all parts of all questions.

1 Here are five problems that computer users can experience. For each one, state a way of preventing the problem.

Problem	Solution
Electric shock	
Backache	
Monitor radiation	
Wrist ache	
Neck ache	

(5 marks)

2 (a) Explain what is meant by repetitive strain injury (RSI).

.... (2 marks)

(b) Explain how a computer user might be subject to RSI.

.... (2 marks)

3 State three reasons why the extensive use of computers can lead to anxiety and stress in employees.

....

.... (3 marks)

Score   /12

C **These are GCSE style questions. Answer all parts of the questions.**

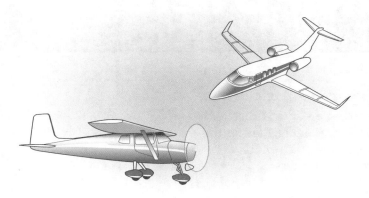

1 Two planes are on a collision course at high altitude. One of them has an on-board computer system that detects the danger and instructs the pilot to go higher. The other plane has no such system and relies on ground-based air traffic controllers to plot a safe path.

(a) Explain why this is a potentially dangerous situation.

....

.... (2 marks)

(b) It is possible for a plane to fly under the control of its own **and** ground-based computers.

   (i) Describe **two** reasons why this could improve safety.

   ....

   .... (2 marks)

   (ii) Describe **two** reasons why this could reduce safety.

   ....

   .... (2 marks)

   (iii) Explain why such computer systems have to be run in real-time mode.

   ....

   .... (3 marks)

2 An organisation employs many computer users who complain that they are suffering from eye strain. State **three** ways that the organisation can help to reduce this problem.

....

....

.... (3 marks)

Score   /12

How well did you do?

0–9   Try again
10–14 Getting there
15–24 Good work
25–29 Excellent!

TOTAL SCORE   /29

**For more on this topic
see pages 76–77 of your Success Guide**

COMPUTER MISUSE

A

Choose just one answer, a, b, c or d.

1 It is more difficult to keep data secure on a computer system than in paper files because
(a) computer data can be easily copied
(b) passwords are easy to guess
(c) all computer data can be read by hackers
(d) encrypted data is easily read by hackers.
(1 mark)

2 An employee may be concerned about personal data being held on the company's computer system because
(a) the data may be erased
(b) the data may be used to calculate pay
(c) the data may be viewed by unauthorised people
(d) the data may be irrelevant.
(1 mark)

3 An employee copies software from his employer's network. This is illegal because it is
(a) hacking
(b) infringement of copyright

(c) damaging to the company's data
(d) compromising the network's security.
(1 mark)

4 A school buys a site licence for a software product. This means that
(a) the school can make copies of the software and give it to the students
(b) the school is entitled to free updates
(c) the software can be used anywhere in the school
(d) the school can only use the software on certain machines.
(1 mark)

5 The police want to see what websites a person has been visiting. Their best source of information would be
(a) the user's hard disk
(b) the records of the websites concerned
(c) the user's ISP
(d) the telephone company's records.
(1 mark)

Score /5

B

Answer all parts of all questions.

1 Fill in the gaps.

There is lots of .... stored on computer systems about everybody. The supermarket may have details of your .... and the local authority knows about your .... Your place of work stores details about .... and .... which makes it possible for .... to find out how much .... they can take off you.
(7 marks)

2 Give three reasons why computer technology increases risks to the public of invasion of privacy.

....

....

.... (3 marks)

3 State three items of information that a school might hold about a pupil.

....

....

.... (3 marks)

Score /13

C These are GCSE style questions. Answer all parts of the questions.

1 Rosie has taken out a hire purchase agreement to buy some furniture. She is asked to fill in a form, which includes many personal details. The details will be stored on a computer file. State **two** reasons why she may be concerned about her details being on a computer file.

....

.... (2 marks)

Only Registered Users Receive Technical Support, Product Updates, New Product Offerings.

SUPER MAIL Version 3.1
SERIAL No 601254689

SOFTWARE LICENCE FORM
SINGLE USER LICENCE

MR☐ MRS☐ MS☐

First Name   Last Name

Company

Address

City   Postal Code

Country   Phone Number

E-MAIL

2 (a) Explain what is meant by a software **licence**.

....

.... (2 marks)

(b) Explain what is meant by a **site licence**.

.... (1 mark)

(c) Explain why the **unauthorised copying** of software can be harmful to all computer users.

....

.... (2 marks)

3 An employee in a large insurance company has to use computers in his work. He has to sign a **code of conduct**.

(a) Explain what a code of conduct is.

.... (1 mark)

(b) State four problems that a code of conduct is designed to overcome.

....

....

....

.... (4 marks)

Score   /12

How well did you do?
0–10 Try again
11–15 Getting there
16–25 Good work
25–30 Excellent!

TOTAL SCORE   /30

For more on this topic see pages 78–79 of your Success Guide

75

DATA PROTECTION ACT

A

Choose just one answer, a, b, c or d.

1 The Data Protection Act forbids the passing of personal data
  (a) to a third party under any circumstances
  (b) outside the European Union
  (c) to the data subject
  (d) to a third party without the data subject's permission. (1 mark)

2 A person whose details are stored on a computer system is called a
  (a) data user   (c) data protection registrar
  (b) data subject   (d) systems manager. (1 mark)

3 A person who stores details about another person on a computer system is a
  (a) data user   (c) data protection registrar
  (b) data subject   (d) systems manager. (1 mark)

4 Which of the following is a part of the Data Protection Act?
  (a) data must be the minimum required for the purpose
  (b) data must only be used for accounting purposes
  (c) data must not be used for direct mailings
  (d) data must be as complete as possible (1 mark)

5 The Data Protection Act covers data which is stored
  (a) on computer systems and paper systems
  (b) on computer systems only
  (c) on paper systems only
  (d) for accounting purposes only. (1 mark)

Score /5

B

Answer all parts of all questions.

1 Which three of these categories of data are not subject to the Data Protection Act?

Category	Tick three boxes
Spreadsheet documents	☐
Police records	☐
Security service records	☐
Customer account details at a bank	☐
Medical records	☐

(3 marks)

2 In terms of the Data Protection Act, explain what is meant by the term data subject.

.... (3 marks)

3 In terms of the Data Protection Act, explain what is meant by the term data user.

.... (2 marks)

4 Fill in the blanks.

Organisations that hold personal data about individuals must register their details with the

.... , who is a person appointed by the .... to keep records of such organisations. (2 marks)

5 List three rights that data subjects have under the Data Protection Act.

.... (3 marks)

Score /13

C **These are GCSE style questions. Answer all parts of the questions.**

1 Stephanie bought a computer games machine. She filled in a registration form to activate the guarantee. One month later, she received several e-mails advertising new games from several different companies.

(a) Explain why this may be in breach of the Data Protection Act.

....

.... (2 marks)

(b) When challenged, the company claimed that they had done nothing wrong. How could they justify this claim?

....

.... (2 marks)

(c) Stephanie wondered what other details they had stored about her. Explain how the Data Protection Act could be used to reassure Stephanie that no further details were on file.

....

.... (2 marks)

2 Joe has been earning extra money and not paying tax on it. He is surprised to find that the tax authorities find out about this. Explain why this is not regarded as illegal under the Data Protection Act.

....

.... (2 marks)

3 (a) A census is carried out. Every person is required to give the census authorities data, some of which is personal. Explain why this is not a problem under the Data Protection Act.

....

.... (2 marks)

(b) Explain why doctors can sometimes be exempt from the provisions of the Data Protection Act.

....

.... (2 marks)

Score   /12

How well did you do?

0–10   Try again
11–15   Getting there
16–25   Good work
26–30   Excellent!

TOTAL SCORE   /30

For more on this topic see pages 80–81 of your Success Guide

USING THE INTERNET

A **Choose just one answer, a, b, c or d.**

1 Which of these protocols is used by mobile telephones to access Internet pages?
 (a) FTP (c) IPX
 (b) SMP (d) WAP (1 mark)

2 Web pages contain instructions about how the text is to be displayed. The instructions are embedded in the page as
 (a) hyperlinks (c) anchors
 (b) tags (d) frames. (1 mark)

3 A small program designed to run in a web page is called
 (a) a hyperlink
 (b) an anchor
 (c) an applet
 (d) a frame. (1 mark)

4 A website makes use of multimedia. This means that it contains
 (a) moving pictures, text and sound
 (b) text and images
 (c) applets and scripts
 (d) hyperlinks and scripts. (1 mark)

5 A person often wants to download music from the Internet but finds it too slow. The best way to reduce download times would be to
 (a) change to a different ISP
 (b) install more RAM
 (c) install a broadband connection
 (d) increase hard disk space. (1 mark)

Score /5

B **Answer all parts of all questions.**

1 (a) Home computer users need to sign up with an organisation before they can use the Internet. What is the name of this type of organisation?

.... (1 mark)

(b) These organisations often provide additional services beyond just making a connection. State four other services commonly offered by such organisations.

....
.... (4 marks)

2 (a) Some organisations provide high bandwidth links to the Internet. Explain what is meant by bandwidth.

.... (2 marks)

(b) (i) State one method by which a high bandwidth link may be provided for a user.

.... (1 mark)

(ii) What additional hardware will be required to connect the computer with this link?

.... (1 mark)

3 Most Internet users want to use e-mail. Describe two distinct ways that e-mail software can be made available to a user. Give an advantage of each.

....
.... (4 marks)

Score /13

78

C These are GCSE style questions. Answer all parts of the questions.

1 **(a)** The picture below shows a web page as seen on a computer. The labels point to some typical features visible when viewing a web page.

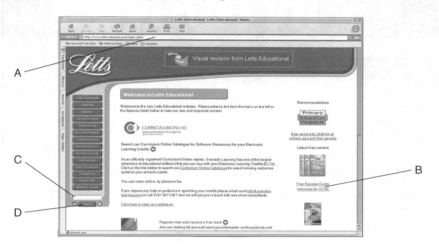

Complete the following table by selecting the correct letters for each of these features.

Feature	Letter
Command button	
Text box	
Hyperlink	
URL	

(4 marks)

(b) What type of software is used to produce this web page display on the user's computer?

.... (1 mark)

2 Lou is planning to set up a website to advertise his car repair business. He already has a PC and the normal peripherals that come with a PC. He needs to set up his pages using a coding system that all web pages use.

(a) What is the name of this code?

.... (1 mark)

(b) What type of software will he need to help him make web pages without having to write all the code himself?

.... (1 mark)

(c) Lou connects his computer to the Internet by using an extra piece of hardware. What is the name of this hardware and why does he need it?

....

.... (4 marks)

Score   /11

How well did you do?

0–9	Try again
10–14	Getting there
15–24	Good work
25–29	Excellent!

TOTAL SCORE   /29

For more on this topic see pages 84–85 of your Success Guide

FEATURES OF THE INTERNET

A

Choose just one answer, a, b, c or d.

1 Web pages contain instructions about how the text is to be displayed. The instructions are embedded in the page ask
(a) anchors   (c) tags
(b) hyperlinks   (d) frames.   (1 mark)

2 Which of these instructions, embedded in a web page, would cause the text following it to be displayed in the largest letters?
(a) <HEAD>   (c) <TITLE>
(b) <H6>   (d) <H1>   (1 mark)

3 When a web page is completed, it can be uploaded onto a host server by using
(a) FTP
(b) HTTP
(c) SMP
(d) IPX.   (1 mark)

4 An advantage of using web-based e-mail software over e-mail software installed on your own computer is
(a) more files can be attached
(b) mail is downloaded more quickly
(c) larger attachments can be sent
(d) mail can be accessed from any connected computer   (1 mark)

5 An enquiry using a search engine produces too many 'hits', but a way of narrowing down the search is to
(a) put the enquiry in quotes
(b) use fewer words to search for
(c) try a different search engine
(d) choose a search engine with '.com' in its address.   (1 mark)

Score   /5

B

Answer all parts of all questions.

1 Here is part of the HTML code for a web page.

```
<html>
<head>
<title>Programming in C#</title>
</head>
<body bgcolor="#ffffff">
<h1>Programming in C#</h1>
```

(a) Explain what HTML stands for and what it does.

.... (2 marks)

(b) The code contains special markers in angle brackets such as <h1>. What are these markers called?

.... (1 mark)

(c) Explain the purpose of these markers ....

.... (2 marks)

2 Web pages usually contain hyperlinks. Explain what a hyperlink is.

.... (2 marks)

3 Explain what a search engine is.

.... (2 marks)

Score   /9

80

C **These are GCSE style questions. Answer all parts of the questions.**

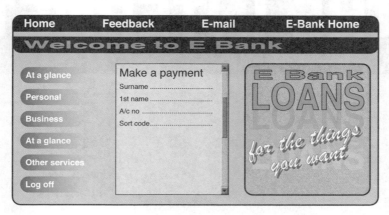

1 (a) Capital and Counties Bank has introduced an on-line banking service. State **three** advantages to customers of this service.

....

....

.... (3 marks)

(b) State **two** advantages to the bank of introducing this service.

....

.... (2 marks)

(c) Lyn is a customer of Capital and Counties Bank. She is interested in using the service, but she is worried about hackers.

(i) Explain what is meant by **hacking**.

.... (2 marks)

(ii) State **three** ways in which the bank can guard against hacking.

....

....

.... (3 marks)

2 A holiday company has started advertising cut-rate holidays on the Internet. Explain how they are able to offer holidays at a reduced rate by this means.

....

.... (2 marks)

Score   /12

How well did you do?

0–8	Try again
9–13	Getting there
14–22	Good work
23–26	Excellent!

TOTAL SCORE   /26

For more on this topic see pages 86–87 of your Success Guide

THE INTERNET

A

Choose just one answer, a, b, c or d.

1 HTML documents are particularly designed to be displayed by a
(a) DTP program
(b) browser
(c) word processor
(d) text editor. (1 mark)

2 Connecting a computer to an ISDN line requires the use of a
(a) modem
(b) hub
(c) router
(d) switch. (1 mark)

3 An organisation that provides access to the Internet for customers is called
(a) ISP (c) PSTN
(b) ISDN (d) HTTP. (1 mark)

4 What is the purpose of entering a user ID when accessing an e-mail account?
(a) to improve security
(b) for billing purposes
(c) to make sure that the message travels by the correct route
(d) to direct the user to the correct mail box (1 mark)

5 The coding system used to construct web pages is called
(a) FTP
(b) HTML
(c) HTTP
(d) SMP. (1 mark)

Score /5

B

Answer all parts of all questions.

1 Briefly state what the Internet is.

....

.... (3 marks)

2 (a) Explain what is meant by the term e-commerce.

.... (2 marks)

(b) A company is introducing e-commerce to help its business. State considerations that will have to be looked at to ensure that the e-commerce is a success.

....

.... (3 marks)

3 (a) The Internet uses certain protocols. State what is meant by a protocol.

....

.... (2 marks)

(b) State the protocol used to upload files to a website.

.... (1 mark)

4 Describe the difference between the signals used internally in a computer and those used by many telephone lines.

.... (2 marks)

Score /13

C These are GCSE style questions. Answer all parts of the questions.

1 This is a typical screen for composing and sending e-mails.

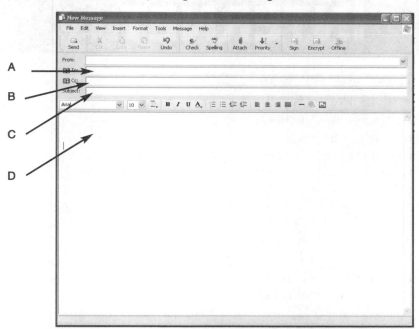

A
B
C
D

(a) Describe the purposes of boxes A, B, C and D.

A ....

B ....

C ....

D .... (4 marks)

(b) On the screen, there is an attachment button. Explain the purpose of this button.

.... (1 mark)

2 (a) Sophie has just switched on her computer. She wants to send an e-mail message to a friend. Describe the steps that she needs to go through in order to send the message.

....

....

.... (6 marks)

(b) Sophie has noticed that she has new mail. One message is from someone she has never heard of. She deletes this mail without opening it. Explain why this is a good idea.

.... (1 mark)

Score   /12

How well did you do?
0–10   Try again
11–15   Getting there
16–25   Good work
26–30   Excellent!

TOTAL SCORE   /30

For more on this topic
see pages 84–87 of your Success Guide

DRAWBACKS OF THE INTERNET

A — Choose just one answer, a, b, c or d.

1 It is possible for private information sent over the Internet to be intercepted by hackers or investigators. An effective way to reduce the risk of this invasion of privacy is to
(a) use encryption techniques
(b) change your ISP regularly
(c) set the browser to disallow cookies
(d) increase the level of security settings on the browser. (1 mark)

2 A moving picture is embedded in a web page. It appears in a small window instead of using the whole screen. The reason for this is
(a) less data has to be sent, therefore making the image quality better
(b) browsers cannot operate full-screen
(c) less data has to be sent, therefore making the movement smoother
(d) less programming is required. (1 mark)

3 Some people are unhappy about using on-line banking. One reason is
(a) the bank is more likely to make mistakes
(b) fear that their details may be accessible to others
(c) the service could cost more
(d) they will not be able to write cheques. (1 mark)

4 Software that is used to stop children accessing unsuitable websites is called
(a) a web browser
(b) encryption software
(c) an applet
(d) a filter. (1 mark)

5 On a web page, a word or image that leads to another location when clicked is called
(a) an anchor (c) a header
(b) a hyperlink (d) an address. (1 mark)

Score /5

B — Answer all parts of all questions.

1 Fill in the blanks.

Many websites contain material that offends people. One way of preventing access to these sites is to .... them using a .... This does not always work, because the websites often change their .... Some websites provide illegally copied software. This is illegal because it is a breach of ....
(4 marks)

2 Someone used a search engine to find websites about London buses. The table shows what words were used for the search (the search string). The search engine reported how many 'hits' or websites were found. The numbers of hits were

• 33,100,000 • 298,000 • 12,300

(a) Match the number of hits against each search string used.

Search string	Number of hits reported
London buses	
"London buses"	
London	

(3 marks)

(b) Explain why the number of hits varied so much.

....

....

....

....

(4 marks)

Score /11

C These are GCSE style questions. Answer all parts of the questions.

1 **(a)** A company has installed Internet facilities for all its staff. The systems manager has found that some of the staff are misusing the facilities. Describe **three** activities that the system manager might consider to be misuse of the Internet facilities and why there might be objections to these activities.

....

....

....

....

....

.... (6 marks)

(b) The company needs to send confidential material to its business partners. Explain why this material should **not** normally be sent by e-mail.

....

.... (2 marks)

(c) The company wants customers to buy from them over the Internet. They are finding that not many customers want to do this. Explain why many people are worried about buying goods over the Internet.

....

....

....

.... (4 marks)

Score   /12

How well did you do?

0–9	Try again
10–14	Getting there
15–23	Good work
24–28	Excellent!

TOTAL SCORE   /28

For more on this topic see pages 88–89 of your Success Guide

BENEFITS OF THE INTERNET

A

Choose just one answer, a, b, c or d.

1 A system of web pages designed for use within one organisation is called
(a) internal mail
(b) an intranet
(c) an extranet
(d) local network. (1 mark)

2 An advantage of using the Internet for research is
(a) the data is always up to date
(b) it is possible to see the latest research
(c) the data is always reliable
(d) the data has been written by experts.
(1 mark)

3 An advantage of e-mail is
(a) it is totally secure
(b) it can be accessed from any connected computer in the world
(c) you only receive the communications that you want
(d) it costs nothing to send. (1 mark)

4 It is a good idea to limit the amount of graphics on a web page. Which of these facts is relevant?
(a) most surfers have small amounts of RAM
(b) some surfers use ISDN
(c) some surfers have broadband connections
(d) most surfers use modems. (1 mark)

5 An advantage of shopping over the Internet is
(a) a wide range of goods to choose from
(b) prices are always less
(c) the suppliers are always reliable
(d) sending money over the Internet is secure.
(1 mark)

Score /5

B

Answer all parts of all questions.

1 Fill in the blanks.

Businesses use the Internet to advertise. Sometimes they make use of multimedia, which combines
.... , ... and .... in the display. These displays are often presented as small applications, called .... , which can be embedded in the web page.
(4 marks)

2 (a) List three advantages to shoppers of shopping over the Internet.

....
....
.... (3 marks)

(b) List three disadvantages to shoppers of shopping over the Internet.

....
....
.... (3 marks)

SMART SHOP

FRED's SPORTS SHOP

3 Not everyone is able to take advantage of the benefits of the Internet. Give three reasons why this may be the case.

....
....
.... (3 marks)

Score /13

These are GCSE style questions. Answer all parts of the questions.

1 A university student is doing research for an assignment on photosynthesis. He has decided to use the Internet to help him.

(a) Give **three** reasons why the Internet might be more helpful in doing research than using printed documents.

....

.... (3 marks)

(b) What type of Internet service will help the student to find what he wants as quickly as possible?

.... (1 mark)

(c) Some of the information that he finds is of no help to him. State **two** reasons why this might be the case.

....

.... (2 marks)

(d) Describe how he could make sure that the information is reliable.

....

.... (2 marks)

2 (a) State **three** ways in which the Internet can help businesses.

....

....

.... (3 marks)

(b) Some businesses maintain their own internal web-based information systems.

(i) What's the name of such a private system?

.... (1 mark)

(ii) State **two** ways in which such a private web-based information system could be of use to the business.

....

.... (2 marks)

(iii) Explain why such a system could produce extra expense for the business.

....

.... (2 marks)

Score   /16

How well did you do?

0–11   Try again
12–17 Getting there
18–29 Good work
30–34 Excellent!

TOTAL SCORE   /34

**For more on this topic
see pages 90–91 of your Success Guide**

MIXED GCSE-STYLE QUESTIONS

1 Bloggs & Co has installed a local area network (LAN) that has a star topology. Fred is the network manager.

(a) Explain how a network of computers can be an advantage over several stand-alone computers.

....

.... (2 marks)

(b) On a separate piece of paper draw a diagram to show how computers are arranged in a star topology. (3 marks)

(c) Explain why a star topology is often preferred to a bus topology.

....

.... (3 marks)

(d) Explain the difference between a client computer and a file server in a LAN.

....

.... (3 marks)

(e) Fred is worried that some users might damage the data on the LAN. Explain how Fred can help to reduce this risk.

....

.... (3 marks)

2 A company is planning to introduce an e-business department to supplement its existing activities. Goods are to be advertised and sold on-line to customers via the Internet.

(a) Describe **three** ways in which workers may be affected.

....

.... (3 marks)

(b) Describe **three** ways that the business might benefit from this.

....

.... (3 marks)

(c) Describe **three** ways that customers might benefit.

....

.... (3 marks)

(d) Explain why some customers might be unwilling to use the on-line purchasing facilities.

....

.... (2 marks)

(e) Describe how the company could take action that would reassure customers.

....

.... (2 marks)

(f) The company sets up a database of customers. This database includes customer names and addresses. When an order is being sent, the database software prints a label.

The systems flow chart below shows the whole of this process. Label each item in the flow chart. Use the following statements:

- customer table

- key in customer number

- label

- print label

- search customer table.

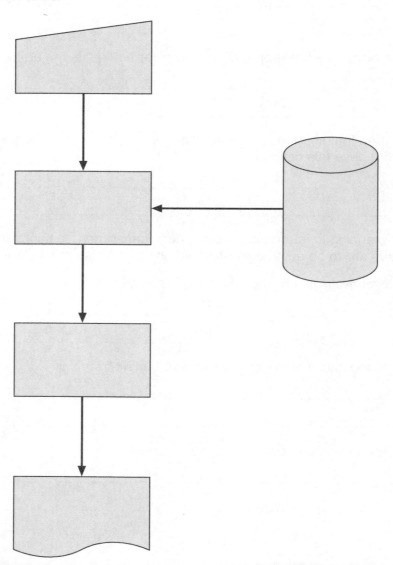

(5 marks)

3 A firm of solicitors often communicates with other firms and their clients using e-mail. They send some of their legal documents as attachments.

(a) Explain **three** advantages that e-mail has over ordinary mail.

....

....

.... (3 marks)

(b) Describe why the solicitors might prefer using e-mail instead of making a telephone call.

....

.... (2 marks)

(c) It is possible to encrypt e-mails. Explain what is meant by encryption.

....

.... (2 marks)

(d) In some countries, it is illegal to encrypt e-mails. Outline arguments for and against this restriction.

....

.... (2 marks)

4 Rashid is looking for information to help him complete a geography project about weather. He has collected a lot of data about rainfall and temperature in his own area. He wants to compare his data with similar data from other countries. He has access to computer facilities.

(a) What software would he need to produce some graphs of his weather data?

.... (1 mark)

(b) Explain how he would use this software to do this.

....

.... (3 marks)

(c) Rashid wants to enter the names of the months in a column. Explain how he can do this without typing every one.

.... (2 marks)

(d) Explain how he could find out the information he needs about conditions in other countries.

.... (2 marks)

(e) Describe why this information might be unreliable.

.... (2 marks)

(f) Describe how he could ensure that the data was as reliable as possible.

.... (1 mark)

5 Capital and Counties Bank is introducing an on-line service. Customers can log on to a website and examine their balances, make payments and set up standing orders.

Each customer has a security number. This is made up from their date of birth, followed by a year code that indicates the year when they opened their account. An extra digit is produced by a calculation and added at the end.

(a) Explain why this number would be unsuitable for use as a key field in the bank's database.

.... **(1 mark)**

(b) Explain what is meant by data validation.

....

.... **(3 marks)**

(c) Explain how a range check could be used to validate the reference number.

.... **(2 marks)**

(d) What's the name of the extra digit at the end of the reference number?

.... **(1 mark)**

(e) Explain how the extra digit at the end of the reference number can help reduce errors.

....

.... **(3 marks)**

6 (a) Explain the difference between a computer simulation and a computer model.

....

.... **(2 marks)**

(b) A model is used to predict the effects of flooding in a river. Explain why, in this case, a computer model is useful.

.... **(2 marks)**

(c) One year, after abnormal rainfall, the flooding is particularly worse than predicted by the model. Explain why the model may have failed to predict the consequences.

.... **(2 marks)**

7 Which **two** of these are examples of utilities found as part of an operating system?

(a) a driver for a CD re-writer ☐

(b) a wallpaper file ☐

(c) a database ☐

(d) a database management system ☐

(e) a spell checker ☐

(f) a disk defragmenter ☐ **(2 marks)**

8 Which **two** of these tasks are suitable for batch processing?

(a) producing exam grades at an examination board ☐

(b) producing pay slips ☐

(c) displaying fuel consumption to a driver ☐

(d) navigating an aircraft ☐ (2 marks)

Total score /72

MIXED QUESTIONS – ANSWERS

1 (a) can share data, share software, share hardware, communication between users, can work at any workstation (any two points)

(b) server at centre, separate cables to, many workstations arranged around server

(c) fewer data collisions, faster performance, greater reliability, as each workstation has its own connection to server/hub/switch (any three points)

(d) client is where user works, place where user logs in, server is where files are stored, shared facilities located, handles requests from clients, maintains network security, network services (any three points)

(e) put users into groups, allocate rights according to need, make some files read-only, hide some files, backup data

2 (a) need retraining, may be made redundant, may need new staff, new skills required, more job security, more job satisfaction (any three points)

(b) more customers, lower overheads, more trade, better image (any three points)

(c) wider range of goods/services, faster service, lower costs, no need to travel to buy (any three points)

(d) worry about loss of privacy, on-line fraud, hackers getting credit card details, prefer to deal with real sales staff (any two points)

(e) install firewall, to prevent external access to files, encryption, to make intercepted data meaningless (any two points)

(f)
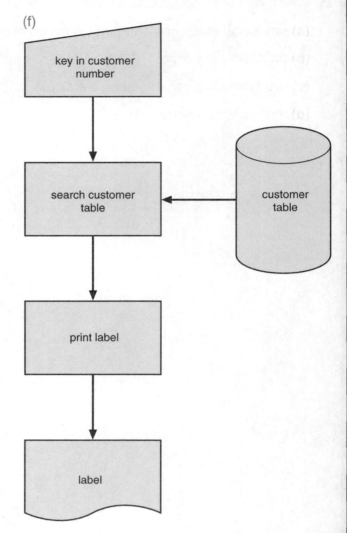

3 (a) faster delivery, can be accessed anywhere, cheaper to send than ordinary mail, can send attachments, mailing lists, carbon copy feature, keeps records (any three points)

(b) don't have to wait to find the person, can send information at own convenience

(c) data is scrambled/enciphered, so that only those with the key can understand/decrypt it

(d) For restriction: can intercept criminal/terrorist communications, help reduce crime.
Against restriction: personal freedom/privacy, the state controls enough of our lives as it is.

4 (a) spreadsheet

(b) enter data into cells, highlight range, access graph utility/wizard, enter labels/headings (any three points)

(c) enter first month, fill down/use autofill

(d) e-mail a contact, get data as an attachment, look up data on websites (any two points)

(e) contact might not have accurate equipment, know how to use it, data may be out of date (any two points)

(f) choose website with care, check date when last updated (any one point)

5 (a) this could produce duplicates

(b) data checked by computer/software, at time of entry, that it falls within limits/is reasonable/acceptable

(c) date of birth part can be checked, to ensure that it is a possible date

(d) check digit

(e) arrived at by calculation, when entered again – calculation repeated, if not the same, error reported, any error likely to be picked up (any three points)

6 (a) simulation is a representation of real life situation, model is mathematical rules representing situation, simulation is based on model (any two points)

(b) many different variables can be tried, in a short time, unusual situations can be tried (any two points)

(c) data may have been inadequate, rules may have been in error, extreme conditions not tested (any two points)

7 a, f

8 a,b